SCOTLAND

Edited by Steve Twelvetree

First published in Great Britain in 2003 by
YOUNG WRITERS
Remus House,
Coltsfoot Drive,
Peterborough, PE2 9JX
Telephone (01733) 890066

All Rights Reserved

Copyright Contributors 2003

SB ISBN 1 84460 290 7

FOREWORD

Young Writers was established in 1991 as a foundation for promoting the reading and writing of poetry amongst children and young adults. Today it continues this quest and proceeds to nurture and guide the writing talents of today's youth.

From this year's competition Young Writers is proud to present a showcase of the best poetic talent from across the UK. Each hand-picked poem has been carefully chosen from over 66,000 'Hullabaloo!' entries to be published in this, our eleventh primary school series.

This year in particular we have been wholeheartedly impressed with the quality of entries received. The thought, effort, imagination and hard work put into each poem impressed us all and once again the task of editing was a difficult but enjoyable experience.

We hope you are as pleased as we are with the final selection and that you and your family will continue to be entertained with *Hullabaloo! Scotland* for many years to come.

CONTENTS

Roo Kerr (11)	1

Airth Primary School, Falkirk

Emma Crews (11)	1
Jodie Cherubim (11)	2
Elaine Davidson (11)	3
Lisa Bell (11)	3
Emma McLachlan (10)	4

Antonine Primary School, Bonnybridge

Nicole Knox (10)	4
Gemma McConkey (10)	5
Michelle McAlpine (10)	5
Fiona McArdle (10)	6
Allanah Gibson (10)	6
Lewis Gordon (10)	6
Scott McCutcheon (10)	7
Kirsty Smith (10)	8

Beaconhurst School, Stirling

Susan Johnston (10)	8
Fraser Sivewright (10)	9
Dominick Dreczkowski (10)	9
Daniel Keith (10)	10
Emma Donoghue (10)	10
Finlay MacBeath (10)	11
Sophie Browne (10)	11
Kirstie Smith (10)	12
Caroline Williamson (10)	12
Ruairidh Moore (10)	13
Iona McIntosh (11)	13
Philippa Inglis (10)	14
Stephanie Hanley (10)	14
Neil McGregor (10)	15
Jacky Stidolph (10)	15
Ruaraidh Ellison (10)	16

Emma Shaw (10)	17
Steven Thomson (10)	18
Charlotte McAfee (10)	18
Rachel Haywood (10)	19
Duncan Carter (10)	20

Carmuirs Primary School, Falkirk

Grant Anderson (10)	20
Ben Barclay (10)	21
Christopher Davidson (10)	21
Jade Wilson (10)	22
Gemma Donaldson (10)	22
Cassandra Robertson (10)	23
Scott Clark (10)	23
Gillian Heeps (10)	24
Janet Ross (10)	24
Connie Williams (10)	25
Stephen Brown (10)	26
Ashley Stirling (10)	26
Kerr Andrew Chalmers (10)	27
Stuart Ashe (10)	28
Shane McConnon (10)	28
Megan Wood (10)	29
Paula Laidlaw (10)	30
Alannah Hall (10)	31

Dalintober Primary School, Campbeltown

Benjamin Ballantyne (11)	31
Charles McFadyen (10)	32
Rachel Conley (11)	33
Heather Lazarus (11)	34
Fiona Mitchell (10)	35
Ewan Millar (10)	36
Fraser Gillespie (11)	37

Drongan Primary School, Ayr

Michelle Stewart (11)	37
Melissa Zienkiewicz (11)	38

Justin Bradford (11)	39
Ainslie Wilson (8)	40
Stacey Caine (8)	40
Laura Woods (10)	41
Gemma McVey (8)	41
Cheryl Barr (10)	42
Martin Johnston (7)	42
Graeme Cassells (11)	43
Louise Wilson (7)	43
Lisa Hutchison (11)	44
Andrew Allison (8)	44
Shivonne Mitchell (11)	45
Louis Jones (8)	45
Ashley Conn (11)	46
Paul Kiltie (8)	46
Ashley Barr (10)	47
Lesley Boyd (11)	48
Laura McPherson (11)	49
Karen Dobie (11)	50
Thomas Milne (11)	51
Lee Borthwick (11)	52
Jennifer Hope (11)	53
Cheryl Corrigan (11)	54
Kimberley Davidson (11)	55
Daniel Dickie (11)	56
Kyle McKee (10)	56
Gemma Payne (11)	57
Jordan Kelly (10)	57
Michelle Milligan (10)	58
Daniel Fitzsimmons (11)	59
David Johnston (10)	60
William Gibb (11)	60
Natalie McCutcheon (10)	61
Keith Cuthbert (11)	61
Sarah Kelly (10)	62
Daryl White (10)	62
Connor Ramsey (10)	63
John Frame (10)	63

Steven Harris (10)	64
Nicole Rose Pirie (10)	65
Shaun Brown (10)	66
Ross Stark (10)	66
Joe Bealing (10)	67
William Hunter (9)	67
Gemma Reid (10)	68
Ross Douglas (9)	68
Johnstone Shearer (10)	69
Jason Alexander (8)	69
Kimberly McPherson (10)	70
John Curtis (9)	70
Coleen Roney (10)	71
Jamie Logan (9)	71
Stewart Armstrong (10)	72
Kyle Campbell (9)	72
Mark McGhee (10)	73
Alistair Stewart (9)	73
Jason Dickie (10)	74
Kevin Cuthbert (10)	74
Shahreen Shah (9)	75
James Jones (9)	75
Stephanie Hewitson (9)	76
Christina Brown (9)	77
Derek Keirs (11)	78
Sarah McTurk (9)	78
Joyce Wilcox (9)	79
George Pringle (9)	79
Claire McPike (11)	80
Natalie Hiddleston (9)	80
John Campbell (9)	81
Vicky McDonald (9)	81
James Fleming (11)	82
Tracy Blackwell (9)	82
Alexa Ferguson (9)	83
Duncan Lucy (11)	84
Jamie Main (9)	84
Paula Greig (10)	85

Megan Rae (9)	85
Kerri Ralph (11)	86
Mark McCubbin (11)	87
James Truesdale (11)	88
Andrew Brown (10)	89
Laura Jess (11)	90
Nicole Forrest (11)	91
Belinda Graham (9)	92

Dunoon Primary School, Dunoon

Phillip Stewart (10)	92
Angela Kirkwood (10)	93
Isla Davidson (8)	93
James Campbell (8)	94
Jack Cleugh (8)	94
Karen Mackay (11)	95
Iain Johnstone (8)	95
Lyndsay Derrett (11)	96
Eilidh Goslan (8)	96
Angela Phillips (8)	97
Claire Clark (8)	97
Katie Thomson (11)	98
Allan Robson (12)	99
Heather Morton (8)	99
Neil McClelland (11)	100
Fraser Davidson (8)	100
Paige Walker (9)	101
Ryan Bogan (9)	101
Lauren Cowan (9)	101
Katie Fletcher (9)	102
Aidan Steel (9)	102
Alisha McMillan (9)	102
Hannah Gray (10)	103
Leah Campbell (9)	103
Richard A Shea (11)	104
Laura Stewart (10)	104
Shona Hamlet (11)	105
Samantha Campbell (11)	106

Meghan Clark (10)	107
Mhairi Cameron (11)	108
Jenna Cushley (11)	109
Michelle Campbell (10)	109
Garry Baird (11)	110
James Tato (11)	111
Michael McArthur (11)	112
Megan Flaherty (9)	113
Jennifer Finlayson (9)	113
Nikki Goffin (10)	114
Scott Johnstone (9)	114
Gillian Downie (10)	115
Hannah MacPherson (10)	116
Hazel Galloway (10)	117
Cian Bennett (8)	117
Katriona Maclean (10)	118
Leanne Frace (10)	119
Morgan Elliott (10)	120

Duror Primary School, Appin

Shannon Hanson (10)	120
Jack Moffit (8)	121
Hannah Malcolm (10)	121
Ben Moffit, Jessie Blanchard & Claire Chrystal (10)	122
Carol Salmon (10)	122

Fallin Primary School, Fallin

Leah Tetstall (9)	123
Louise Boyle (9)	123
Aaron Hazel (9)	123
Kevin Cochrane (9)	124
Abbie Rixon (9)	124
Johnny Hunter (9)	125
Boab Thomson (9)	125
Shauni McGregor (9)	126

Forehill Primary School, Ayr
Shaun Blackwood (11)	126
Lisa Raftery (11)	127
Robert Walsh (11)	127
Laura Williamson (11)	128
Grant Hoggitt (11)	128
Calum Brough (11)	129
Chloe Young (11)	130
Stewart McLellan (11)	131
Heather Carrington (11)	131
Ruaraidh McPike (11)	132
Ian Longworth (11)	133
Nicola Stirling (11)	134
Laura Alexander (11)	135
Mairead McCrossan (11)	135
Melissa Hewitson (11)	136

Kilchrenan Primary School, Taynuilt
Aron Wright (9)	136
Emma Gillespie (8)	137
Chloe Wilkie (9)	137
Callum Leitch (8)	138
Calum Galbraith (9)	138
Jade Sutherland (10)	139

St Andrew's RC Primary School, Falkirk
Dylan Baty (8)	140
Amy Doyle (9)	140
Aidan Buhrmann (8)	141
Claire Williamson (9)	141
Mairead Cowling (9)	141
Rachel Doherty (9)	142
Ruth McElroy (8)	142
Carolyn Paterson (8)	143
Liam Bruce (8)	143
Hannah Jamieson (8)	144
Claire Callaghan (8)	144
Sean Cowell (8)	145

Gavin Cullen (9) 145
Dominic Hamilton (9) 146

St John's Primary School, Ayr
Lauren Douglas (11) 146
Rebecca Shields (11) 147
Sarah Hainey (11) 148

St Mark's Primary School, Hamilton
Lewis Mair (9) 148
Brogan McKendrick (8) 149
Ami Smith (11) 149
Jonathan Lennon (9) 150
Stuart McPherson (9) 150
Charles Kirk (10) 151
Suzanne Hunt (11) 151
Michael McMonagle (10) 152
Scott Hart (11) 152
Colette McKale (10) 153
Martin Scott (10) 153
Mark Russell (9) 154
Stephanie Kirkwood (11) 154
Michael McGuckin (12) 155
Danielle Bryant (10) 155
Grant Kelly (10) 155
Linzi Carty (10) 156
Charlie Reilly (11) 156
Mark Lennon (9) 157
Christopher Brownlie (10) 157
Leigh-Ann Todd (9) 158
Kayleigh Currie (10) 158
Lauren Steven (9) 159
Luke Hill (11) 159
Natalie Webster (10) 160

Sandbank Primary School, Dunoon
Sarah Tait (8) 160
Kiri Newbery (9) 161

Alexander Pearson (8)	161
Vahri McGeoch (9)	162
Emma McDougall (8)	162
Simon McVicar (8)	163
Owen James (9)	163
Kirstin Campbell (8)	163
Donna McFarlane (10)	164
Conor Gillan (9)	164
Ged Preston (10)	165
Mairi Tait (9)	165
Tiffany Robinson (9)	166
Camilla Smith (9)	166
Ryan Scott (10)	167
Andrew Gault (9)	167
Gemma Dorward (10)	168
Iona McNab (9)	168
Callum Barr (8)	169
Liam Jaques (10)	169
Briony Docherty (11)	170
Jenny Jaques (11)	170
Cara Phillips (10)	170
Emily Fairclough (10)	171
Stuart Gilmer (11)	172

Skipness School, Tarbert

Sophie Elder (10)	172
Emma Henderson (11)	173
Aimee Elder (11)	174
Jenny Richmond (10)	175

Southend Primary School, Campbeltown

John Bateman (9)	175
Ashleigh MacMillan (9)	176
Stuart McConnachie (10)	176
Carlyn MacMillan (10)	177
Craig McKerral (11)	177
Natalie Smith (10)	178
Karen Semple (11)	178

Jason Graham (9)	179
Calum Houston (10)	179
Rosie Fraser (9)	180
Rachel Forrest (10)	181
Fiona McKerral (9)	182
Laura Cameron (9)	183
Kerri McCorkindale (11)	184

The Poems

SWIMMING

Swimming is fun!
Swimming is great!
With your best friend
Or wonderful mate!

Maybe breaststroke,
Then butterfly,
And when it comes to a race
I'll really fly!

Roo Kerr (11)

HITLER'S BACK

I'll walk through the forest at midnight tonight,
And try to fight the monsters and fright,
It's very dark,
On the tree ahead of me there's a mark on the bark,
What can it be? I cannot see,
I want someone to help me.
I touch the mark and fall to the ground
All I can see is Hitler staring at me
Bombs fall on the ground
It's like World War III just for me
Hitler's back to fight again
He thinks he's the best
When as you can see he's no stronger than me
I'm back home now, that was very strange
I will never go in that wood again.

Emma Crews (11)
Airth Primary School, Falkirk

EVERYDAY HEROES

There is an unnatural stillness.
when all around there are sirens wailing,
debris falling,
people screaming.
A rush of figures
like a blanket being drawn across the road.
Running, but as if in slow motion.
You can almost hear their hearts beating,
their courage and determination,
which urges them on.

The don't hear the windows crashing;
they don't see the bricks falling,

They only see the people running
needing their help.

With fearlessness they pull people
from the building.

Every day they are heroes,
they are the NYFD.

Jodie Cherubim (11)
Airth Primary School, Falkirk

THE MAGIC BOX

On the table sits the little box
It is very small with a little lock
It is green and gold in colour
Of its kind, there is no other.

It is too good to be true
And whenever I feel blue
I look to it for inspiration
Soon I'm filled with fascination.

My box means a lot to me
I think it's made of magic, see
To hear it is a special thing
When I look inside, it starts to sing.

Elaine Davidson (11)
Airth Primary School, Falkirk

MEMORIES

There are 101 memories in my box,
My very first step when I was young,
My very first word when I was about one,
When I put the star on the Christmas tree
for the first time,
When I started school and didn't like it.

My box is a light mahogany colour,
When you open it,
a ballerina appears and dances,
It stands on my unit so I can always see it,
I'll shut my box quickly
so my memories don't blow away.

Lisa Bell (11)
Airth Primary School, Falkirk

THE CHINESE BOX
(Based on 'Magic Box' by Kit Wright)

In my box . . .
Is the music of Chinese New Year,
The flowing of the dragon's back,
The shape of the lady's beautiful almond-shaped eyes.

In my box . . .
Is the walk of the Emperor,
The feeling of happiness,
The dance of the girls with their long, flowing dresses.

In my box . . .
Are the cherished words spoken in Chinese,
The ancient Chinese traditions, that are still followed today,
The joy and happiness of Chinese New Year.

Close the box, I don't want the magic to disappear.

Emma McLachlan (10)
Airth Primary School, Falkirk

THE MOON IS . . .

The moon is
a round ball sailing through the sky
The moon is
a shining light on black paper
The moon is
my favourite thing in the night sky
The moon can be silvery, golden, red or pink
The moon can be full or waning
The moon is
an ever changeable thing.

Nicole Knox (10)
Antonine Primary School, Bonnybridge

My Little Puppy

The midnight sun puts on a show
For my little puppy down below,
Under ribbons of shining light,
My puppy hugs you and says goodnight.

He likes to gnaw on his juicy bone
While leaning on a big grey stone,
He tugs and pulls his squeaky toy
You know he's such a good boy.

My little puppy runs around
And never likes to be found,
Try and catch him then you'll see
He's as quick as a busy bee.

Gemma McConkey (10)
Antonine Primary School, Bonnybridge

Beach

Sand as soft as cotton wool

Fish as colourful as the rainbow,

Pebbles as smooth as the palm of your hand

Sun as hot as burning fire,
Sea as clear as crystal
Trees as tropical as fruit

Sandcastles as tall as skyscrapers.

Michelle McAlpine (10)
Antonine Primary School, Bonnybridge

AT THE BEACH

At the beach children build sandcastles on the sand
and play skipping hand in hand,
collecting shells in their buckets
and watching waves roll in from the sea.
Children playing merrily,
as the sun slips away
to return another day.

Fiona McArdle (10)
Antonine Primary School, Bonnybridge

NOT A SOUND

There's not a sound in the street
only the wind blowing gently in the night.
There's no sound of animals above or below
only the sound of leaves rattling like they are playing
a game of tig.
The light shines brightly on the ground
and on the ground, nothing can be found.

Allanah Gibson (10)
Antonine Primary School, Bonnybridge

HAVE A CUP OF TEA

There was an old lady from Settle,
Who put on the kettle,
And said, 'Please feel free
To have some tea,
But I only have cups
Made of metal.'

Lewis Gordon (10)
Antonine Primary School, Bonnybridge

MY KITTEN CUDDLES

I have a lovely kitten,
Who is black and white,
We get on so well together,
Because we've never had a fight!

Because she is so irresistible,
I'd never give her away,
I sleep with her, cuddle her,
Every single day.

I would take her to school,
if I could,
Everyone would want her to play,
Maybe I should!

I gave her a name,
it is Cuddles,
I think her favourite hobby,
Is splashing around in puddles.

Now Cuddles,
has reached the age of 4,
She is still a kitten,
Nothing more.

She is everything,
She's the top pet,
She is very nice,
Don't forget!

Scott McCutcheon (10)
Antonine Primary School, Bonnybridge

THE SUN

The sun is a blazing beam of light,
That does not shine in the night.

How calm it could be as I peacefully sleep,
Or as rough as a vicious cat.

But oh how I wish I could go to the sun,
But all my hopes are dashed
as it was just a dream.

Kirsty Smith (10)
Antonine Primary School, Bonnybridge

CUTE AND CUDDLY ANIMALS

Animals are cute and animals are cuddly,
Even in the hallways
You may see a few.
There are all sorts of animals
Living in this world.
I like all animals
Especially horses, cats, puppies, and whales.

There are animals on land
And animals in slinky seas.
We love all animals like our own pets.
All our animals
Are nice
And cuddly.

Susan Johnston (10)
Beaconhurst School, Stirling

MY FAMILY

My mum means everything to me,
She makes my breakfast, lunch and tea
And *always* tells me how much she loves me!

My dad means everything to me,
He's big and tall and very strong
And teaches us from right and wrong.
He also tells me how much he loves me!

My brothers mean everything to me,
We sometimes fight, but we play a lot
And I don't know where I could be or
What I would do without them.
Although they don't tell me, I know they love me!

My pets mean everything to me,
I have two cats and one dog called Millie,
I know they love me!

My family means everything to me!

Fraser Sivewright (10)
Beaconhurst School, Stirling

DRAKE THE SNAKE

There once was a man called Jake,
Who was fooling around with a rake,
Then met a grass snake called Drake,
And got tired and jumped in a lake!
He got out and started to eat cake,
Then went home and started to bake,
But instead wanted a steak!

Dominick Dreczkowski (10)
Beaconhurst School, Stirling

EINSTEIN'S BROTHER

Einstein had a brother
a brother like no other
he went around in clunky shoes
and snored like a drill when he had a snooze.

He smashed down walls
and took great falls
he took a huge stride
across a space very wide

Albert Einstein achieved great fame
but never mentioned his brother's name
he never mentioned *Frank Einstein!*

Daniel Keith (10)
Beaconhurst School, Stirling

WHAT'S THAT NOISE?

What's that noise up in the trees?
It's rustling in the leaves,
It might just be the breeze.

What's that noise in the house?
It wouldn't be a louse,
It might just be a mouse.

What's that noise in my room?
It's not Mum with the broom,
Am I going to my doom!

In my room I find . . . my brother!

Emma Donoghue (10)
Beaconhurst School, Stirling

THE RAINFOREST ANIMALS

Birds whistling in the trees
above the green rainforest leaves.
Small rustles among the forest trees
As leaves fall gently on my knees.

Monkeys swinging through the trees
hiding from the big chimpanzees.
Gorillas after cheeky monkeys
eagles swooping down for prey.

Colourful toucans singing to each other
a tapir looking for its mother.
Macaw, hummingbird, blue morpho butterfly
I see above with glint of sky.

The rainforest is just full of life,
although there is some strife.
A more magical place I cannot imagine,
we must look after this natural treasure.

Finlay MacBeath (10)
Beaconhurst School, Stirling

MY DOG AND HIS WIFE

My dog is brown and white
and you would never guess his delight
to get out his golden flute
and play it with all his might.
He said to his darling wife, 'Oh what is your delight?'
'My delight is to dance round the garden
while you play so light.'
'Really,' he said, and they danced and they danced
all through the night.

Sophie Browne (10)
Beaconhurst School, Stirling

THE GHOST

G remlins are even scared of ghosts
H ere, there, everywhere!
'O oo, I hear something
S ounds like a ghost,' says the girl in her bed.
'T oo late to disappear,' says the girl, 'I have already
S een you!'

'A nd I see you when you are sleeping,' says the ghost
'R ound the house I go, corner to corner
E verywhere, that's right!'

'E verywhere?
V ery creepy, says the girl.' He repeated saying
'E verywhere, everywhere
R oaming around the house.' One day the girl said . . .
'Y es,
W hy not?
H ere I am looking as scary as
E ver'
R emember me when somebody says
E verywhere.

So what?

Kirstie Smith (10)
Beaconhurst School, Stirling

ROLLER COASTERS

Roller coasters are great
Roller coasters are fast and furious.
Roller coasters make you sick
When you come off them
You feel dizzy.

Caroline Williamson (10)
Beaconhurst School, Stirling

THE SKI TEAM

    Have you
             heard of
                      the
                team
              that
          ski?
      Yesterday
they
   got
       victory,
               on
                      the
                 Slalom
              at
          Glencoe.
    Through
   the
   deep
    powdery
    snow.

Ruairidh Moore (10)
Beaconhurst School, Stirling

ONE SPRING DAY

A spring day, all the animals are born.
Spring animals born is a beautiful sight.
Flowers bud.
Lambs skip.
One spring day.
One spring night.

Iona McIntosh (11)
Beaconhurst School, Stirling

BUBBLES

Bubbles are fun
They make you happy
So the best thing to do
When you're feeling blue
Go and get bubbles
And sit on the step
And blow some bubbles
Lovely bubbles.

Bubbles are great when
You don't have a mate
So go and give them a try
They're only fifty pence
And make people stare
Until all the bubbles
Disappear.

Philippa Inglis (10)
Beaconhurst School, Stirling

CUTE

Animals are cute, animals are fun
Rabbits hopping in the sun
Chicks are going *tweet! tweet! tweet!*
The puppy sleeping on the seat

Birds are singing in the trees
While the mouse is eating cheese
Kittens playing with a ball
Running up and down the hall.

Stephanie Hanley (10)
Beaconhurst School, Stirling

A Monster

I saw a scary monster
Staring right at me.
It had big teeth
Like an enormous beast
And a huge tail
The size of a whale!

He was really furry and
Smelt like a curry!
This is what he said to me,
'I want to eat you, I want to chew you,
I want to munch and crunch you!'

I said, 'No way,'
Then I threw a mouse at him
And then he ran away.

Neil McGregor (10)
Beaconhurst School, Stirling

Peep, Peep

Peep, peep go the little birds
Ring, ring goes the bell
Swish, swish go the trees in the wind
Clang, clang goes the clock
Peep, peep, swish, swish go the birds in the trees
Swishing in the wind.
Ring, ring, clang, clang go the bells in the clock.

Jacky Stidolph (10)
Beaconhurst School, Stirling

My Magical Phone

I have a magical phone,
Which has a magical tone,
it sometimes goes *ring*,
and it sometimes goes *ping*,
the tone for my magical phone.

I have one tone for one friend,
and another tone for another,
if I had a brother I'd have a warning tone,
but that's what I have for my mother!

I have lots of games on my phone,
if I lose, I go moan, moan, moan, moan,
I spend all my money,
I'm bad, says my mummy,
the games for my magical phone.

In my magical phone,
there is a long menu of tones,
there's bright sunny meadows,
and black and white zedoes,
the big long menu of tones,
which is all in my magical phone.

Ruaraidh Ellison (10)
Beaconhurst School, Stirling

OUR TEACHER'S MAD

Our teacher's mad,
She has green hair,
She sits all day,
Without a chair!

She likes to sing,
And play the fool,
She took us swimming,
There was no pool!

We do our maths,
She sets hard sums,
And while we're busy,
She sits and hums.

One day last week,
She brought her fox,
It spent all day,
In a large wooden box.

At the end of the day,
She says goodbye,
And with a wink,
Out falls her eye!

Emma Shaw (10)
Beaconhurst School, Stirling

MY EVIL DOG

My evil dog called Tess
She likes to make a mess

Her collar is bright red
She looks so cute curled
Up in her bed

She is a greedy lass
And if you don't move fast
She will grab a bite or two
And will even eat your shoe.

Steven Thomson (10)
Beaconhurst School, Stirling

MY CRAZY FAMILY

First there's Mum, she's a bit dumb!
Next there's Dad, he's quite mad!
Oh yeah there's Tim, he's very dim!
And there's Daisy, she is very lazy!
We have a guinea pig, she likes to dig!
Don't forget our dog or our cat, Mog!
And Tim's fish, he looks delish!
Of course there's me, see me
I'm just Miss Perfect!

Charlotte McAfee (10)
Beaconhurst School, Stirling

THERE IS A PLACE

There is a place inside my head
That I can only see
And this place inside my head
Is full of harmony.

Without war or suffering
Without hunger or pain
Without the lonely crying
But treating people the same.

And that is the place inside my head
That I can only see
And this place inside my head
Is full of harmony.

I wish this world inside my head
You could really see
I wish this world inside my head
Was as real as real could be.

And that is the place inside my head
That I can only see
And this place inside my head
Is full of harmony.

Where you and I could live together
In a happy scene
Where you and I could live forever
'Cause this world is my dream.

Rachel Haywood (10)
Beaconhurst School, Stirling

WHEN SHARKS ARE ABOUT

When sharks are about, don't flop around
Remember don't panic, try to think.
Swim slowly don't splash
Then the sharks won't dash
Don't swim at night or early morning
Check the beach board for any shark warning.
Always swim within the net
Keep your cool or else, swim in the pool!

Duncan Carter (10)
Beaconhurst School, Stirling

CATS AND DOGS

I have four pets
And they are great pets
They are all fun to play with
You can take them and stroke all day long

The dogs are called
Sheb and Rusty
They are my best friends
They never argue or say no

When I take them for a walk
I take them down the park
And they bring sticks back to me

My pets make me happy.

Grant Anderson (10)
Carmuirs Primary School, Falkirk

MY GIRLFRIEND

The moment I looked in her eyes
I began to realise
The beauty and her lovely smile,
I thought she was a pretty child.
I like her shining glasses
And the way we play in the grasses.
She acts like a butterfly
Dancing gracefully through the sky.
Her skin feels like butter
It makes my heart flutter.
Her lovely voice makes me melt
It's the best feeling I've ever felt.
The smell of her hair is so sweet,
I want to sweep her off her feet.
She loves me more than baby sheep
She really makes my heart leap.
Her attitude is so cool,
She's the coolest girl in the school.

Ben Barclay (10)
Carmuirs Primary School, Falkirk

OLD AND NEW

My new pencil tin
My new bedroom bin
My new toy and something
My new PS2 won't go in the bin

My old friends were all boys
My old toys were all for boys
My old friends liked all my toys
My old toys got broken by the boys.

Christopher Davidson (10)
Carmuirs Primary School, Falkirk

My Best Friend Gillian

My best friend is nice.
I wish she liked spice,
She always wears tights.

We always hang out,
She always says she's cute,
She wants to play a flute.

She has a hamster,
It's called Zappy,
It's very snappy.

She has nice hair,
She has a nice chair,
She *disni* like pears.

She worries a lot.
Whit a lassie!

Jade Wilson (10)
Carmuirs Primary School, Falkirk

My Best Friend

Ma best friend is nice,
I wish she liked spice,
She always says she's cute,
I dinney ken what do dae with oot her,

Ma best friend is called Connie,
I wish she had a pony,
I wish a had a collie,
'Cause she is really bonnie.

Gemma Donaldson (10)
Carmuirs Primary School, Falkirk

MY BOYFRIEND BEN

He is very lovely
He makes me laugh a lot
But every time I'm near him
I can't even talk.
I get embarrassed, my cheeks go red
So I have to run away from him
I plan a romantic dinner
Where the lights are low and dim
I can't wait for Valentines
We'll have the perfect day
The perfect love
The perfect couple
Me and my boyfriend
From start to the end
Me and my boyfriend.

Cassandra Robertson (10)
Carmuirs Primary School, Falkirk

FOOTBALL HERO

The football team was playing a game
They were getting beaten, oh what a shame.
Half-time whistle, the ref calls out
Now back on the pitch they all shout.

Running after the ball and falling down
They look just like a bunch of clowns
Running around the goals
Trying to score a goal
Owen's off with a shout
As he gets called out!

Scott Clark (10)
Carmuirs Primary School, Falkirk

My Hamster

My hamster is called Zappy,
He is very yappy.
Zappy makes me happy,
Until he's naughty.

Zappy is so funny,
He loves it when it's sunny.
I wish he'd live forever,
I guess it will never happen.

I love him so much,
He loves my friendly touch.
I make my hamster feel good,
Even when I'm in a bad mood.

Gillian Heeps (10)
Carmuirs Primary School, Falkirk

My Kitten

Kittens, kittens, I love kittens,
I have a teddy, one wearing mittens.
My kitten is such a cutie,
But she chewed up my sister's bootie
She bites, she scratches,
She chews up matches.
She makes an awful mess!
She is such a pest,
But I still think she's the
Best!

Janet Ross (10)
Carmuirs Primary School, Falkirk

MY FAMILY

There's my little pesty brother,
And my skinny little sister,
And a small little brother
Who is cute.

There's my cool tall mum
With two tattoos
And her belly button pierced.

There's my step dad
With loads of tattoos
And big gold rings
That weigh a ton.

There's my aunty pushing the pram,
With Zoe crying for Alan's sweets.
My aunty is tall
With short dark hair.
So everyone beware.

Then there's my doggy
So cute and cuddly.
Her name is Poppy,
I love her so much.
You should have seen her
When she was a pup.

There's my best friend Gemma
She likes to climb up trees.
She always skins her knees
She's a tomboy and sometimes full of joy.
There's my granny and grandad
Who I love much better.
I live with them.
My granny and my grandad
Make sinks and come home with cuts.

Connie Williams (10)
Carmuirs Primary School, Falkirk

THE GHOST OUTSIDE THE PUB

When I was walking to the shop,
I saw the strangest thing.
A big old farmer, with a rake,
But he wasn't in the human race.

I heard stories about ghosts,
But now I know they are real.
He just stared at me,
And I just stared at him.

When I went past him, to look again,
I saw he was gone.
When I got home, it just struck me.
I had seen a ghost!

So then it started, my search for ghosts,
I never met one again.
The strangest thing of all is that,
I still feel that ghost watching me!

Stephen Brown (10)
Carmuirs Primary School, Falkirk

MY KITTEN!

I have a kitten called Socks,
I got him when I had the chicken pox.
He climbs up curtains and rips clothes,
And also has a little pink nose.
He makes a mess,
And likes to sleep in my mum's dress.
But you know what.
I still think he's the
Best!

Ashley Stirling (10)
Carmuirs Primary School, Falkirk

LONG LOST TEDDY

I once owned a teddy bear,
Left it lying on the stairs,
I know my sister hid it,
But cannot find out where.

I hesitated for a moment,
I felt that I wanted to cry,
I didn't know where she'd hidden it and why?
I looked everywhere, then gave a sigh.

I crumpled up paperwork, looking through drawers,
I searched everywhere, under beds,
In dolls' houses, in her toy cradle.
I said to her, 'I give up,'
I felt like I was about to erupt.

Finally I stopped and thought,
Has she's hidden it in her cot?
So I looked, but it was not,
Then maybe I'd forgot . . .

To look under the covers of the cot.

It had got from the stairs,
To there.

My sister was caught,
The search was over,
My mum smacked her bot,
And sent her to Dover.
Goodbye.

Kerr Andrew Chalmers (10)
Carmuirs Primary School, Falkirk

THE WINTER SNOW

The snow goes right in your shoes
You're freezing, *brrrrrrrrrrr*, it's freezing outside
But still you love the snow
You get to fling snowballs, build snowmen
But the snow will go soon
Because it's not everlasting snow, of course.
The bad thing is it's *frrrrrrreeeeeeeezzzzzing*
The good thing about it is you know
Christmas is here.
That's the winter snow for you.
So don't go daft with the snow, be safe.

Oh the winter snow, oh the winter snow
Don't be so cold but more people like it than others
People don't even like the snow
So it's better to get more snow
But less cold.

Stuart Ashe (10)
Carmuirs Primary School, Falkirk

FOOTIE IN THE PITCH

The team ran out onto the park
The sun's gone down, it's getting dark.
'We have to win,' the captain says
To play for the Cup in a couple of days.

Winning the game is what we want
Lots of goals, the fans all taunt
The ball goes into the back of the net
We're going to win this game. I bet!

Shane McConnon (10)
Carmuirs Primary School, Falkirk

LITTLE FISH

My name is Little Fish,
I live in a seaweed dish,
I'm really scared of the shark,
Who lives in the sunken Noah's Ark,
I'm tired of being a puny fish,
To be a dolphin is my wish,
Not like a clown fish, juggling clams,
Nor slimy skin, like sea snail Sam.

Dolphins really love to dance,
I wish I had the chance,
To be like a dolphin with each glance,
But no, I'm just Little Fish,
Who lives in a seaweed dish,
Who's really scared of the shark,
Who lives in the sunken Noah's Ark,
I am just a puny fish,
Who has a silly dolphin wish,
Who doesn't want to be like sea snail Sammy,
Nor his clown fish friend called Clammy.

Megan Wood (10)
Carmuirs Primary School, Falkirk

THE ANIMALS I LIKE

I don't like fat cats
I hate small rats
But I adore great
White sharks
they are blue
and white and
they look about
for food at night.
fish is their
dish for the
evening and
they are thieving
they steal from
other sharks
and they swim
about waiting
for their bait
often they have
to wait and wait . . .

Paula Laidlaw (10)
Carmuirs Primary School, Falkirk

MY FAMILY

I have a brother and he's such a bother.
He eats custard with yucky, bright mustard
and does nothing but
be annoying all day.

See my mum, all she does is suck her thumb.
She eats jelly and gets a wobbly belly
and thinks dogs
are big and smelly.

My dad is so cool
but he acts the fool.
and he plays jokes on me
when I come home from school.

Alannah Hall (10)
Carmuirs Primary School, Falkirk

DRAGON FIGHT

Fire is all around me
The dragon's flames surround me
His eyes are glistening in the night
And suddenly he flies a great height.
He is soaring in the air
Up there without a care
I throw my sword up to its head
He flies left and right, but I hit him. He's dead.
He hits the ground,
With a mighty sound.
Yes! I win.

Benjamin Ballantyne (11)
Dalintober Primary School, Campbeltown

THE WORST DRAGON

The worst dragon lives in a cave
attacked only by soldiers so brave.
He eats and gobbles everything up
it wouldn't surprise me if he threw up.
Even when he is asleep
he still makes your heart skip a beat.

When he kills you for pleasure
he'll take all your treasure.
Once he's done that
he'll eat your cat.
Red boiling fire comes from his belly
too bad he just won't watch telly.
Soldiers attack with big long pikes
but their bodies just end up on spikes.
Today he attacked our village
he had the best privilege.

'Die, die, die!' shouted the dragon
as he set fire to a wagon.
'Run, run, run!' Shouted someone
'No,' said the dragon, 'I'm having fun!'
After that we decided to attack
With our weapons at the back.
Great luck was ours
as the dragon fell on top of our flowers.
On that very day
on the 4th of May.
Never again
will we be troubled in vain.

Charles McFadyen (10)
Dalintober Primary School, Campbeltown

FEELINGS

Angry
Sometime feelings show,
There is a wrong and right.
Most people know,
When you have been in a fight.
The facial expressions tell all.
Stay on the good side of right,
Next time you play ball,
You won't get a fright!

Sad
Sometimes feelings show,
Just ignore them right.
If they pick on you,
Just close your eyes really tight.
Let the tears stream down,
And let them feel the guilt,
You can't help it if you're not
Very well built.

Happy
Sometimes feelings show,
Always stay on the bright side.
Keep smiling on,
Some rules you don't have to abide.
There may be something wrong,
Don't let it take its toll.
Just always remember,
Sometimes feelings show.

Rachel Conley (11)
Dalintober Primary School, Campbeltown

THE DREAM

I went to bed at nine o'clock,
Oh no, school tomorrow! I thought.
I dozed off quite quickly and began to dream . . .
The snow began to fall,
Eventually there was a blizzard,
Then I woke up and went back to sleep,
Dream on . . .
In the morning I woke with snow all around me.
That's strange! I thought and then looked up.
The roof was gone and I wasn't in bed,
'Where am I?' I'm cold, my hands are numb and red,
My teeth began to chatter and then I realised,
Then I woke up and went back to sleep,
Dream on . . .
All of a sudden I was wrapped up warm,
With a scarf, a hat, gloves and my cosy coat on,
I was outside in my garden,
The drive was blocked,
Snow! Yeah! No way I can get to school! I thought.
I went round to the shed and got out my sledge,
'This is fun!' I shouted as I went up and down the hill,
All day I played until the day was done.
Then I woke up,
It was only a dream!

Heather Lazarus (11)
Dalintober Primary School, Campbeltown

THE KEY FITS

The key fits!
Trembling,
I turn the lock . . .
What's inside?
Is it a monster
That will eat me up?
Will it be more homework?
It might be something nice like,
Mmmmmmm . . . chocolate!
It could be something I really hate . . .
My big brother!
It might be a faraway land,
It could be *Mrs Glendinning*.
Ready to give me a year's time of school work!
I'm ready to open it . . . No I think I will open it later!
I'm frightened!
I'm shaking in my boots!
I'm turning the lock
I have unlocked it!
I just need to pull the handle . . .
. . . and it's, it's a . . .
New baby sister!

Fiona Mitchell (10)
Dalintober Primary School, Campbeltown

THE KEY FITS

The key fits,
Trembling,
I turn the lock . . .
What will await me
As I open the door?
Will it be trouble
Or will it be a pet patrol?
I'm shaking, shaking like a fish on a plate
Hopefully it will be something I don't really hate.
What awaits me, what awaits me?
What awaits me, what awaits me?
What's going to happen to me?
Suddenly I have second thoughts.
Shall I turn it or shall I not?
I've got to face my biggest fears
Turn it till I get tears.
Gradually I turn it,
And it's . . .
My mum with a bad hair day
Oh no, she must have lost her curling brush!

Ewan Millar (10)
Dalintober Primary School, Campbeltown

SCHOOL FOOTY

Neil throws the ball up
Up in the air
Scally controls it
Then to Naughton
Passed it to DJ
Then *clunk*, Campbell goes straight through
DJ, then Ian, running blowing the whistle.
Free kick to DJ
Crosses it in the box like Beckham
It was a scramble
Then up front player
Gillespie scores
Goal!

Fraser Gillespie (11)
Dalintober Primary School, Campbeltown

MY FANTASY LAND

My fantasy land would be full of chocolate.
My fantasy land could be jelly.
My fantasy land could be called Marshmallow Land.
My fantasy land would be sunny all the time.
In my fantasy land the people would be kind all the time.
In my fantasy land there would be no school.
In my fantasy land there would be nice hills to sit on for picnics.
In my fantasy land you could do anything
In my fantasy land chairs would be made of clouds.
In my fantasy land the beach would be made out of
                                      chocolate and jelly.
My fantasy land, I wish could come true.

Michelle Stewart (11)
Drongan Primary School, Ayr

IN MY ROOM

In my room, late at night
When I'm asleep the socks all fight.
In my room, when I'm in bed
My shoes dance beneath my bed.
In my room, if it's past eleven
My ripped up toys come down from heaven.
In my room there is something strange
How many bouncy balls jump from toy planes?
In my room, it was weird
How all my socks have disappeared.
In my room, my board games move
And my disco tapes start to groove.
In my room, it's quite a shock
To hear my jumper's married a clock
In my room, my CDs sleep
And every time they snore they give a little peep.
In my room, my wardrobes speak
In a little language they call bleak.
In my room, my paints all race
To see who will win first place.
In my room, where it's nice and peaceful
Until a toy chases another for its place on the shelf.
In my room, it's very quiet
Now I'm out of the room . . . and they start a riot!

Melissa Zienkiewicz (11)
Drongan Primary School, Ayr

WHEN I GO ON HOLIDAY

When I go on holiday
I jump out of my bed.
When I go on holiday
I get ready as fast as I can.
When I go on holiday
We put our suitcases in the car.
When I go on holiday
We head to Glasgow airport.
When I go on holiday
We have to take our suitcases to the desk.
When I go on holiday
I go and get a comic.
When I go on holiday
I look at all the planes.
When I go on holiday
I jump on the plane
When I go on holiday
We all sit down in the plane.
When I go on holiday
I can't wait to go to the hotel.
When I go on holiday
I meet lots of friends.
When I go on holiday
I don't want to go home.

Justin Bradford (11)
Drongan Primary School, Ayr

VIKINGS

Vicious Vikings living in a village
with their villagers.
Along come some villains
trying to steal their gold.
Imagining they were fierce,
But they knew they weren't.
Kidnapping people for slaves.
The King of the Vikings wants to kill the slaves.
But the others won't let him.
Impossible as can be
And they know it is.
Nasty Vikings fishing for something to eat,
But they can't catch anything.
Greedy Vikings go out to sea
To try and get some gold.
But the people won't let them have any
So they go home with no gold.

Ainslie Wilson (8)
Drongan Primary School, Ayr

VIKING

V icious Vikings are looking out for gold.
I   nteresting Vikings looking for gold.
K illing people in raids.
I   nhabiting their lands.
N orway and Sweden, Vikings come from.
G old is very special.

Stacey Caine (8)
Drongan Primary School, Ayr

CHRISTMAS STOCKING

What will I find in my Christmas stocking,
When I put my hand in?
Will I find toys?

A book, a top,
A grocery shop,
A box of beads for me,
Some sweets too,
A dolly, some holly,
A white turtle dove,
And maybe some love,
A flower for Mum,
A tie for Dad,
An orange, a penny,
But not too many
A big silver star
On the top.

That is what I will find.

Laura Woods (10)
Drongan Primary School, Ayr

VIKING

V ikings thumping through the village.
I nterested in sailing for gold and silver.
K illing people that are bad people.
I mpossible to be true in the world.
N asty, nasty Vikings in one small village.
G old and silver armoured Vikings.

Gemma McVey (8)
Drongan Primary School, Ayr

AUTUMN

Autumn morning I wake up
with leaves falling from the trees
beige, russet, chocolate and chrome.
When prowling cats come out to roam.

I smell some smoke when I awake,
is it a fire or a badly burnt cake!
Days are shorter and flowers fade,
when feral birds come out to play.

I see some squirrels and hedgehogs too
I hear some children shout 'Toot-a-loo!'
when they set off for school,
all wrapped up they look really cool.

I'm inside all wrapped up
with my blanket and my cup full of tea.
My mum made it,
especially for me.

Cheryl Barr (10)
Drongan Primary School, Ayr

VIKING

V icious Vikings live in Scandinavia.
I gnorant Vikings looking for gold.
K illing people and getting slaves.
I nto the dark, creepy woods looking for wood.
N asty Vikings making a lot of noise.
G reediest killers in the world.

Martin Johnston (7)
Drongan Primary School, Ayr

GLUTO FROM PLUTO (AN ALIEN)

Gluto is from outer space.
He has a very mean looking face.
His home planet is Pluto.
And his mother's name is Bluto.
He has very furry hair.
Even furrier than a bear.

He has silver steel claws for hands.
Which are strong enough to break steel bands.
He has two antennae on his head.
Which are very glowy and red.
He has 12 tentacles that are long and slimy.
And his gold razor blade teeth are very, very grimy.

And last but not least his blue jelly-like body.
Is protected by silver plated armour
That looks quite ploddy.

Graeme Cassells (11)
Drongan Primary School, Ayr

VIKINGS

V ikings were impossible to beat.
I nto the deep sea Vikings sailed.
K idnapped people in raids.
I nland, every Viking was hunting for gold and silver.
N ever been back in their longboats for raids.
G iant Vikings searched the villages.

Louise Wilson (7)
Drongan Primary School, Ayr

AUTUMN

All the weak leaves start
to fall off the trees with a sway,
That's autumn.

I like autumn best of all
because of the different shades of yellow, red and brown,
That's autumn.

Flowers fade away and all
the robins and squirrels come out to play,
That's autumn.

In autumn, clocks go back
and it starts to get dark early,
That's autumn.

Lisa Hutchison (11)
Drongan Primary School, Ayr

VIKINGS

V icious Vikings living in a village, sailing the seas
      waiting for an attack.
I nteresting, ignorant Vikings, not so happy,
      very nasty.
K illing, torturing, stabbing, raiding, looking for gold and
      silver, maybe weapons.
I njured villagers are made, happy Vikings
      rich as rich can be.
N asty Vikings raiding again and gain. Stealing from other
      Vikings.
G reedy Vikings go to raid again, steal from the rich.

Andrew Allison (8)
Drongan Primary School, Ayr

BONFIRE NIGHT

On Bonfire Night the fire is bright,
It's a wonderful sight,
All cats and dogs get a fright,
It's Bonfire Night.

Fireworks go off one by one,
Set the bonfire, watch it burn,
All cats and dogs run,
It's Bonfire Night.

Children get sparklers,
From their mums and dads,
Fireworks are dangerous,
It's Bonfire Night.

The rocket went bang,
Where there was a gang,
Then there was a banger,
It's Bonfire Night.

Shivonne Mitchell (11)
Drongan Primary School, Ayr

THE VIKINGS

V icious Vikings killing people and stealing from villages.
I ll-treating people and killing everyone, the Vikings
K illing and stealing from everyone, vicious Vikings
I n war with everyone and no one will fight the Vikings.
N o one dares to fight the Vikings, the Vikings killing everyone.
G iant Vikings and small Vikings stealing from everyone.

Louis Jones (8)
Drongan Primary School, Ayr

FIREWORKS

Fireworks are very noisy
I get a fright in the night
Because they go *boom*, *bang* and *splash*.
In the night.

Fireworks are very colourful and bright.
My dog gets a fright in the night.
My dog goes *woof* and lets out a squeal.
In the night.

Fireworks are dangerous
But when I can't go to a fireworks display
I get furious.
In the night.

Ashley Conn (11)
Drongan Primary School, Ayr

VIKING

V icious Vikings looking for a new land, Vikings stay in Scandinavia.
I gnoring what the other people say, invading new territory, getting all the money.
K illing all the people that get in the way, monks hiding all the money.
I nto the longboat with the dragon head.
N asty Vikings fighting for their country, noisy Vikings, thinking they're smart.
G agging people and chopping off their heads, stealing gold from other lands.

Paul Kiltie (8)
Drongan Primary School, Ayr

PRUTO FROM PLUTO

Hi, I am Pruto from Pluto
You know the planet don't you?
Well I am here to play football
And no one knows it's me, Pruto from Pluto.

I sit here on the bench
Wanting to go out and play
Watching everybody every single day
And no one knows it's me, Pruto from Pluto.

I have green and white hair
And all the children stare
I have a blue nose and a green body
But I don't care
And no one knows, it's me, Pruto from Pluto.

With my metal arms and legs
And my 20 fingers and toes
I have a great kick
But I never get picked
And no one knows it's me, Pruto from Pluto.

I have green and white teeth
And some rocket jet trainers
Which people think are weird
And no one knows it's me, Pruto from Pluto.

I am 1000 years old
I support Celtic and I have a Celtic strip
That is what I wear all the time
I have three eyes and four ears.

I finally get to play, I shoot, I score
And no one knows it's me, Pruto from Pluto.

Ashley Barr (10)
Drongan Primary School, Ayr

An Hour Before The Game

An hour before the game
I'm feeling a bit weak and lame.
Looking at my bowls
Wondering if there's holes.
15 minutes to go
the clouds are down low
Do you think I'll win?
If I do, what will I win?

Now it's time to play the game
Up to twenty-one wins the game.
I'm in pain in my brain
Now we've started I'm up eight.
Will I get beat?
On and on we play the game
Now I'm up nineteen - zero.
'Excited, excited I am.'

'I won, I won, yes, yes.'
Twenty-one - one was the score.
My back is sore
with bending over.
I'm showered in prizes galore.
Yesss!

Lesley Boyd (11)
Drongan Primary School, Ayr

JUG-A-LUGS FROM JUPITER

My name is Jug-A-Lugs.
I have a mohican, it is blue
I have a red nose
It is as long as a hose.
I don't really like to pose.
I have 6 arms and legs
My fingers are shaped like pegs.
I have 5 eyes on the back of my head
I have 5 eyes on the front of my head
My teeth are half purple, half blue
I have an orange body
And I have jug ears.
I get fire coming out of my nose.
I have spikes on the back of my head
But they are *invisible*.
I sit at the corner of a room
Where nobody can see me.
I have no friends
They all shout and bully me
Who oh why did I have to be
Jug-A-Lugs from Jupiter?

Laura McPherson (11)
Drongan Primary School, Ayr

THE BULLY

I see the bully waiting for me
Will he hit me? Wait and see,
For he's big and I'm small.
But that doesn't mean anything
At all to him.

I wish I could find someone.
Someone who wants to have fun
But that job, I think it won't be done.
Then again I am only this mess
That couldn't care less.

He'll follow me to my house
Just like a little mouse.
I wish someone would phone
But I'm all alone
By myself.

People shut the door in my face
Everywhere I go they know who I am.
I feel like I'm in a jam
Because I feel so
Afraid.

When I walk home by myself
I wish I could hide on a shelf
Or maybe move away
To get away from
The bully.

Karen Dobie (11)
Drongan Primary School, Ayr

THE NEW TEACHER

My new teacher was weird
When he first appeared
and he had a hairy beard
and his name is Mr Feard.

My new teacher is sad
and sometimes he is bad
He calls me his little lad
if I'm not bad.

My new teacher has a home
with a little toy gnome
and some bath foam.

My new teacher has a pleat
and size 11 feet
He is quite neat.

My new teacher has got a big lip
he took us on a good trip
and he gave me a little nip
and a little tip.

My new teacher is big
I think he wears a wig
and talks like a pig
and he likes to play tig.

My new teacher likes baths
he talks a lot in maths
he goes for walks on little paths.

Thomas Milne (11)
Drongan Primary School, Ayr

THE BIG MATCH

When I was eight years old.
I started playing for a football team.
I got new football boots
And I got new goalkeeper gloves.
When I went to play my first game,
I was really nervous.
Oooh dear!

I played on Astroturf for my first game.
My team were on first, I let a goal in
And my mum said, 'Oooh that's a shame.'
So I got in a panic and thought,
I'm no use to anyone.
My team said, 'Unlucky.'
Oooh dear!

I'm on again, the referee blows his whistle
I'm shaking and my legs are like jelly
And so is my belly.
I'm standing in my nets.
A shot came in, I just saved it, *Yes*!
I did it, I saved it, people started clapping.
Oooh Yes!

My last game, I'm kind of better.
So here I go.
That's it started, I'm concentrating hard
A shot's coming hard, I can catch it,
No! No! No!
Honestly don't be a goalkeeper!
I'm rubbish.

Lee Borthwick (11)
Drongan Primary School, Ayr

MERVICKY

My name is Mervicky from Mercury
My planet was a bit too hot for me, so I moved to Earth
A place in Scotland called Perth
I've been literally over the moon.

I wear a plastic bag because I drool
All the kids at school call me a fool
Well they're not like me
Mervicky from Mercury.

I'm 1000 years old, that's quite old I'm told
I have a bright pink nose
That is shaped like a hose
64 fingers and toes.

I sit at the side of the class, if 'Who are you?' is asked
Up goes the shout
'There's a monster about!'
and soon the whole world knows.

I've got green fire hair and an evil stare
I have purple teeth
And I'm purple beneath
My quite weird looking clothes.

My name is Mervicky from Mercury
My planet was a bit too hot for me, so I moved to Earth
A place in Scotland called Perth
I think I will go home soon.

Jennifer Hope (11)
Drongan Primary School, Ayr

A Rainy Day

I don't like the damp weather
These dreadful damp, dull days
Your new hairdo getting wild
I hate it when it's raining!

I don't like the dull weather
All dark, grey and gloomy
Looking out of the steamy windows
I hate it when it's raining!

I don't like the dark weather
Waking up to find it's dark
Walking to school in the dark
I hate it when it's raining!

I don't like the clammy weather
Coming to school very cold
Going in it's very warm
I hate it when it's raining!

I don't like the drizzly weather
Especially when I can't go outside
Sitting at the front window
I hate it when it's raining!

Eventually getting out to play
Splish, splash
What good fun
Rain, it's OK!

Cheryl Corrigan (11)
Drongan Primary School, Ayr

MY HOUSE

My house is quite big
It has a smelly fridge
But when I smell the food
It makes me feel good
In my house

When I zoom to my room
I listen to my music
But when I hear a call
I zoom across the hall
In my house

When I run to the bathroom
I have to shut the door
Cause when my little sister
Sees, she lets out a roar
In my house

Out in my garden
I like to play with my friends
But when they score a goal
All you hear is '*goal*'

When I go to my brother's room
I walk in, when I sniff
The smell it makes me hit the wall
In my house.

Kimberley Davidson (11)
Drongan Primary School, Ayr

Rainy Day

On a rainy day
Windows start to steam up
That's what happens on a rainy day.

On a rainy day
People splash in puddles
That's what happens on a rainy day.

On a rainy day
People put on their window wipers
That's what happens on a rainy day.

On a rainy day
The roads are slippery
That's what happens on a rainy day.

On a rainy day
I sing 'Rain, rain go to Spain,
Don't come back here again.'
That's what happens on a rainy day.

Daniel Dickie (11)
Drongan Primary School, Ayr

Football

F oreign teams are a different class,
O n the pitch players give it their best!
O n my 13th birthday my dad's going to take me to White Hart Lane.
T he fans cheer on the players.
B all in the net and all the fans shouting!
A t Ibrox, when an Old Firm game is on, everybody is shouting.
L ate at night the floodlights are on.
L ittle children stand on the seats to see them play.

Kyle McKee (10)
Drongan Primary School, Ayr

Rainy Day

Playing properly in the puddles at the park.
It's a damp, dull, dangerous, dark day.
The clouds are cluttering the sky.
As people are walking by.
It's a rainy day.

It's a horrible heavy day when it's raining.
Flooding onto the floor goes the rain.
Jumping on the ground
Makes a lot of sound.
It's a rainy day.

Camping in the cold country.
Is where we are on a winter's day.
Wet everywhere
and people stare.
It's a rainy day.

Gemma Payne (11)
Drongan Primary School, Ayr

Chocolate

C hocolate is sweet like sugar.
H ot chocolate is good in the winter.
O range chocolate is not good.
C hocolate may contain nut traces.
O range chocolate is my mum's favourite.
L ate at night I steal chocolate out of the fridge.
A ll day I eat chocolate.
T erry's All Gold is fantastic!
E veryone likes chocolate!

Jordan Kelly (10)
Drongan Primary School, Ayr

Moods

I am happy when I am with my mum
I am happy when I have sweets,
I am happy when it is Christmas
And my birthday too.
Moods, moods, moods

I am bored when there is nothing to do
I am bored when I am by myself,
I am bored when it's raining
And when my friends aren't coming out.
Moods, moods, moods

I am excited when I am going to a pop concert
I am excited when my favourite programme comes on,
I am excited when I am going to a party
And when I go out to dinner.
Moods, moods, moods

I am sad when people in my family take ill
I am sad when my pets die,
I am sad when I see the news
Especially all the kidnappings going on.
Moods, moods, moods.

Michelle Milligan (10)
Drongan Primary School, Ayr

AUTUMN

Autumn is a lovely time
all the leaves are coloured
some of them are tawny
just like a buzzard
some of them are cream
which lets out a beam
and then there's yellow
which lets out a bellow
and last of all there's cherry
which looks like a berry.

Autumn is a lovely time
all the animals appear
like little hedgehogs
with a spiky ear
which snuffle through the leaves
or little squirrels
that run across the eaves
and at last there's the rabbit
and they like to grab it.
I love autumn best of all.

Daniel Fitzsimmons (11)
Drongan Primary School, Ayr

THE TERRIBLE TWINS

The twins next door they always fight
They give each other a terrible fright
They fight over who is the biggest and oldest
And their mum just says -
'You're just the same size and age.'

The twins are six now - they still fight!
Their mum just says -
'You're big enough to understand -
You're just too much the same!
Your dad and sister never fight and neither should you!'

The twins are 18 now, they still fight
Their mum has given up!
The twins just carry on fighting -
About who is the oldest and biggest!

David Johnston (10)
Drongan Primary School, Ayr

THAT'S WHERE HE LIVES TO ME

Over the mountains and under the sea
That's where he lives to me.
Under the grass and under the mud
That's where he lives to me.
Above the clouds in the blue sky
That's where he lives to me.
Through the cave and through the dark
What's where he lives to me.
In the walls with all the spiders
That's where he lives to me.
Through my head and through my brain
That's where he lives to me!

William Gibb (11)
Drongan Primary School, Ayr

BEING LATE

Being late for work,
Being late for school,
That is what I'm good at -
Being late for this,
Being late for that!

I can't blame it on the rain,
Or blame it on the train,
I can only blame it on myself -
And going to bed at twelve!

The teacher says I should -
Go to bed a lot earlier,
But I said, 'I don't like going to bed
At nine, ten or eleven.
I love going to my bed at twelve
And being late in the morning!'

Natalie McCutcheon (10)
Drongan Primary School, Ayr

MY BROTHER

M y brother lives in his world of football and PlayStation.
Y esterday he annoyed me all day.

B rothers are pests so say you don't want one.
R ather than a brother have a sister.
O nly brothers are pests and annoy you all day.
T est your brother and keep him busy all day.
H im and his friends are all geeks.
E very night he snores.
R ather sleep in the living room than in the same room as him!

Keith Cuthbert (11)
Drongan Primary School, Ayr

MY WONDERFUL MUM

M y mum is the best in the world,
Y es, she's the greatest!

W hen I'm feeling sad or I'm needing help
    she always comes to my rescue
    and makes me feel better.
O n school days when I'm sick, she gives me hot tea in bed.
N o one can replace her - no one at all!
D oes everything for me and my sister,
E verything I ask her, she always gives me a great answer.
R ight from when I was born she's been right there for me.
F ighting with my mum is something I never do!
U nder my bedclothes, I'm always thinking of her.
L iving with her is a dream come true.

M y mum loves me and I love her.
U nder the roof we play games.
M y mum is the best in the world!

Sarah Kelly (10)
Drongan Primary School, Ayr

THE WEIRD NOISES

It is in the night
When I jump in fright
Because of the weird shaped shadows
All I hear is –
Ooooah! Ooooah!

I turn on my light
And look at the window
And it is the wind that I hear!

Daryl White (10)
Drongan Primary School, Ayr

A Chocolate Alien

A chocolate alien came to invade the earth

C hocolate was his favourite food
H eat would melt him
O r water would melt him too
C ats were not afraid of him
O n the day he landed everyone was scared
L ast week the alien was not there
A ll the people were happy
T uesday the alien came again
E veryone was making a plan

A cat has scared the alien
L ong spaceship he had
I n the town the alien was there
E lephant scared him away and he never came back
N ever did he come again.

Connor Ramsey (10)
Drongan Primary School, Ayr

Feelings

I have feelings, good ones and bad.
I have feelings, happy and sad.
I have happy feelings when I think about my dad.
I have sad feelings when I think about my gran.
My gran lives in America - not China or Japan.
I have sad feelings when I think about my gran.
I have good feelings when I score a goal in the park.
I have angry feelings when I fight with my brother Marc.

John Frame (10)
Drongan Primary School, Ayr

MY GRAN'S DOG

My gran's dog is small but fast.
It is black with brown streaks.
It is a yorkie.
My gran's dog.

Its first name is Toya,
Its second name - Harris of course!
Everywhere I go in the house it follows me.
My gran's dog.

If anyone tries to hurt me it will pounce at them.
It has a basket full of toys, which it always knocks down,
And I get the blame for it!
My gran's dog.

Whenever I see it, it always has a toy in its mouth.
My papa always fights with it.
It always lies at the bottom of your feet.
My gran's dog.

If you take its toys it will jump on you.
Every corner you turn it is sneaking about.
If you lie down it will lick your face.
My gran's dog.

Steven Harris (10)
Drongan Primary School, Ayr

MY FAMILY

First there is my mum
always doing the dishes
she always makes such lovely food
like fruit with raspberry swishes.

Secondly there is my dad
always watching television
his favourite is Allo, Allo
lies and laughs with a ho, ho, ho.

Thirdly there is my dog and cat
always in front of the fire
my dog takes my cat's space
so my cat bites him and
gets its space . . . at last!
Then there is me
as bored as can be
always playing in my room with my friends
we always play pretend
and have lots of carry-ons
so Mum sends us out!

Nicole Rose Pirie (10)
Drongan Primary School, Ayr

WHAT A BROTHER

W hat a brother I've got!
H ow are little brothers nippy?
A brother gets on your nerves.
T errible things my brother does.

A brother is terrible

B rothers can do stupid things
R otten things my brother does
O h no - I shout when he goes off his head!
T he mess is his I say
H e pulls my hair and tugs my clothes.
E h? He says and blames it on me.
R un when you see a little brother!

Shaun Brown (10)
Drongan Primary School, Ayr

ALIENS INVADE

A liens are very cool.
L ate at night aliens attack.
I n the spaceship aliens plan their attack.
E arth is their target to attack.
N ear earth their spaceship lies.
S ilver aliens attack earth.

I would not like to be an alien.
N ight is when they attack.
V ery scared I wait for the aliens.
A t night I can see the glow.
D own under ground they are looking for a way out.
E arth is not under attack.

Ross Stark (10)
Drongan Primary School, Ayr

IN THE ICE RINK

I n the ice rink I go to train to win the game
N ow it's the day as I warm up for the game

T he puck is dropped and the game is under way
H urrying down the ice for the puck -we get it and we score!
E veryone jumping around and going crazy!

I n the break the coach says, 'Are you ready?'
C rait's got the puck, shoots and scores!
E veryone clapping and jumping around!

R oaring and shouting - his mum and sister!
I get scored on and am not happy!
N ow the game is over - we win two/one and I get
      man of the match!
K eeping myself awake in the car, off I go home to my bed!

Joe Bealing (10)
Drongan Primary School, Ayr

THE SNOWMAN

I made a little snowman
With a little thin head
With a little nose and a mouth with a smile as well
The next day he was gone
But he left his tracks
And I followed him in the woods
And I saw thousands of snowmen
And partied all night
Then the snowmen disappeared
And I went home.

William Hunter (9)
Drongan Primary School, Ayr

HOLLY AND SCOOBY - MY DOGS

Holly and Scooby -
My dogs.
Holly is a golden retriever
Big, fluffy and white.
Holly and Scooby -
My dogs.
Scooby is a little scruffy -
I should have called him Scrappy!
Holly is a girl.
Scooby is a boy.
After getting them
I'm now full of joy.
But when I was a little girl
Holly chewed my favourite doll!
I was sad but now I'm happy,
As I love them one and all!

Gemma Reid (10)
Drongan Primary School, Ayr

CHOCOLATE

C hocolate is very scrumptious.
H ot or cold, maybe hard.
O n toast chocolate spread is good.
C hocolate is very delicious.
O range is a flavour.
L uscious it is *chocolate*.
A nd chocolate is the best.
T ime to eat chocolate.
E at, eat all night and day.

Ross Douglas (9)
Drongan Primary School, Ayr

THE FOX

The fox wis walking through the wids
step by step
Watching every step it took
In case men came wae the hounds and horses

It ran back tae its den
In case men came wae their belts and powder
Fur their guns

Hidden in its den
worrying fur its cubs
It heard a *bang* and barking in the distance

The next thing it sees
is a hound coming doon in tae the den
They hive a gid fight
But in the end the fox is no more.

Johnstone Shearer (10)
Drongan Primary School, Ayr

SNOW DAY

S   o when I went to school I was throwing snowballs.
N   ow it was time to go inside.
O   ften, many times it snows.
W inter is not like spring.

D angerous, when you are throwing snowballs.
A   boy was building a snowman.
Y ou can build a snowman.

Jason Alexander (8)
Drongan Primary School, Ayr

MY LITTLE SISTER

M y little sister is soft and cuddly just like a teddy bear.
Y awning in the morning she never slept a wink.

L ying in her pram - I wish I was her!
I n the morning she never gets up and I always call her lazy.
T he devil's name is Kelsey.
T oday she has started to say Kim but instead she says Im.
L aura doesn't want her - always left to me.
E veryone says she is just a cutie-pie.

S he always gets spoilt when we go out shopping.
I love my little sister more than Laura.
S he is always sleeping - never up.
T he little bum is nearly one.
E verywhere I go she always follows me.
R emember I must look after her and care for her.

Kimberly McPherson (10)
Drongan Primary School, Ayr

MY SNOWMAN

There was snow coming
I was going to build a snowman.
I rolled a snowball
To make the head and the body.
I used buttons for
His mouth and eyes
And a carrot for his nose.
I gave him a scarf and a hat.
We played on our snowboards.

John Curtis (9)
Drongan Primary School, Ayr

MY COUSIN

My friend is actually my cousin.
And she is nice.
But when she is angry, I think
She is made with a kind of nippy spice.
Sometimes she can be nice.

Now she is ten
She acts like a hen.
I wish she could stay in a pen.

I sometimes go for her.
And sometimes she calls me.
Or sometimes we don't speak.

Now it is night
I need to go to bed.
Maybe I will tell you her name, maybe not.
But instead I will say goodnight.

Coleen Roney (10)
Drongan Primary School, Ayr

THE SNOWMAN

There was a snowman called Jack Frost
He lived in the snow.
He liked to snowboard
Down big slopes and mountains.
He liked to eat snow
A little boy saw him move his head.
So he ran outside but Jack never moved an inch.
The next day it was hot, he only left his hat.
The boy felt sad.

Jamie Logan (9)
Drongan Primary School, Ayr

ON THE FOOTBALL PARK

O n the park, tension is high.
N obody will miss the game.

T oday is Arsenal v Liverpool.
H yppia will have to do well.
E verybody is excited.

F reddie Ljungberg had better score.
O n the park the turf is good.
O ne mistake and any of the players will punish you.
T hierry Henry had better be on form.
B all in the back of the net!
A rsenal, that's who I will be supporting.
L eeds players will be watching.
L iverpool fans make a lot of noise.

P atrick Viera had better tackle hard.
A ll the players better play well.
R iise had better put good crosses in.
K ill everyone who's got the ball.

Stewart Armstrong (10)
Drongan Primary School, Ayr

SNOWMEN

S nowmen are fun to make
N ow you can make a snowman on a snowy day
O n a snowy day you can have a snowball fight
W hen it's snowing you can make a snow angel
M agic snow is fun to play
E ven on a cold day it's fun to play with the snow
N ight is come, the snow melts away.

Kyle Campbell (9)
Drongan Primary School, Ayr

MY LITTLE BROTHER

M y little brother is a monster.
Y ou call him Keiran.

L ittle he is - tough he is too!
I t helps if he stops hitting.
T uesday is when he goes to gym.
T oday we play together.
L ittle and cheeky.
E gg, he does not like.

B rother he is of mine.
R ight and wrong he can be.
O n his birthday he has an action man cake.
T omorrow he goes to a party.
H e loves to play the Xbox.
E gg he hates, but I like egg.
R ight - my poem is finished!

Mark McGhee (10)
Drongan Primary School, Ayr

SNOW DAY

S now, snow is a fun time
N ow it is time to play until you die
O n snow days it is good fun to play
W hen it is a snow day you can make snowballs

D ay is when you go to play
A nd when it is a snow day you have fun
Y es I said, 'When it is a snow day you make a snowman.'

Alistair Stewart (9)
Drongan Primary School, Ayr

MY LITTLE SISTER

M y little sister – she sneaks into my room and gives
    me a fright!
Y elling and screaming she wakes me up in the morning
    With her feet going *bang! Bang! Bang!* off the wall.

L ittle and skinny is my little sister – hides under my bed
    and even in my toy box!
I t is very funny when she fights with my brother -
    I say to them - '*ha, ha, ha.*'
T he little witch does not let me do anything.
T errorising the house is what she does!
L ittle as well is my brother - he is a pain as well as my sister.
E verybody else thinks she is all right but I think she's a pain!

S o she annoys me and I get angry with her.
I t is funny when she shouts at my brother.
S o I laugh and she hits me!
T hey wrestle on my bed.
E ither me or my brother she bosses about every day.
R unning around after me!

Jason Dickie (10)
Drongan Primary School, Ayr

THE SNOWMAN

S nowmen are fun to make on a cold day.
N ow all the snow is on the ground.
O n a snowy day I play in it all day.
W et and damp when the snow melts.
M ountain sides are covered in snow.
A snowman runs about all day shouting.
N ow it is time to go inside for a cup of tea.

Kevin Cuthbert (10)
Drongan Primary School, Ayr

MA WEE SCOTTIE DOG

Ma wee Scottie dog I called
It wee Rabbie, its
Always barking here an there an everywhere.
It even opened the door for me.
When I got back fae ma pal's hoose, I
Can tell ya now it's no sa wee
Cas it's nearly as big as me. Aw
Ma pals laughed at me.
Cause ma wee Rabbie was nearly
As big as me!
'Och well,' I said 'it's no ma
fault he eats too much.'
He even ran out the
Back garden and ate a wee bird.
Then came in and ate ma dinner.
I think he eats whatever he sees.
But I'm telling ye now wan a these days
He's gonnae be bigger than the hoose.
But sad to say he wandered away
An a don't ken how a lost ma wee Scottie.

Shahreen Shah (9)
Drongan Primary School, Ayr

A SNOWY DAY

There was one snowy day
And it was a school day
When I got to school
There was snow everywhere
There were snowballs flying in the air
Everywhere people were running about with laughter
And having a good time.

James Jones (9)
Drongan Primary School, Ayr

SNOWMAN

One winter's evening it had been snowing
So I went outside to play with my brother.

We had snowball fights and we were sliding.
My little brother said, 'Let's build a snowman.'
I said, 'Why not!'

So we started building the snowman
First we made his body
Then the head and used buttons
For his eyes and nose.

When we turned away to go in the house
It started snowing
We laughed and went inside
And shut the door.

A couple of days later the snowman melted
My little brother was crying
But we said, 'Snow melts,
It's fun when it lasts.'

After a while he calmed down
And took me upstairs to play with me.

After that we went for a walk
To my grandpa's and played the computer.

Stephanie Hewitson (9)
Drongan Primary School, Ayr

THE SNOWMAN

There was a snowman
And his name was Frosty.
He liked to play and jump around.

He had a hat
He had a nose
He had eyes and a mouth.

Then a little boy came out
To see his little snowman
He went back in his house.

He turned around,
He saw the snowman move.
He stood and watched him,
Then he stopped.

When the little boy turned around
The snowman started dancing about.
Then all the snowmen came over the fence.

They all danced together.
The they all lived
Happily ever after.

Christina Brown (9)
Drongan Primary School, Ayr

MY ROOM

My room is blue.
I sit in it.
It is a fun place for me and you.

I play PlayStation in my blue room.
I play games on it.
My music goes boom.

In my blue room I have a teddy
My gran bought him for me.
I call him Eddie.

My blue room is a place for me and my friends to go.
We listen to music.
My mum usually says, 'No!'

Derek Keirs (11)
Drongan Primary School, Ayr

MY WONDERLAND

In my wonderland, promise you won't laugh.
I have a box head dog, it really makes me sad.
He hops about all morning.
He hops about all night.
I have another problem
He ran away last night.
I chased him up the back roads.
I chased him down the hill.
I ran about the waterside
And fell into the well.

Sarah McTurk (9)
Drongan Primary School, Ayr

ALIEN

My friend is a little alien
His name is Rob
I like to call him Zeroyd
But he doesn't like it much
He lived on Mars
He lives with me now
He likes to sleep in my cupboard
And he likes to jump and shout
Then one quiet night
He rolled across the floor
He went crazy and started to shout
He said his friends came to see him
Then my mum went crazy
As they slid around the floor
When I woke the next morning
I found he wasn't there
And I never saw him again.

Joyce Wilcox (9)
Drongan Primary School, Ayr

MY SNOWMAN

One day I got out of bed
I looked out of the window
There was snow everywhere
I got changed and ran outside
I got a snowball and rolled it
And it got bigger and I made
A snowman.

George Pringle (9)
Drongan Primary School, Ayr

LOSING MY FIRST LOVE

The moment I saw you.
Those shiny brown eyes.
That shiny dark hair.
That some would despise.

But when I overheard you
I didn't think it could be true
You were leaving me
Leaving me for somewhere new.

But if I could change
One moment in time
It would be when you kissed me
Kissed me goodbye.

The time has changed
I've got to move on
But I'll think of you
Forever on.

Claire McPike (11)
Drongan Primary School, Ayr

DANCING

D ancing Queen is someone who's dancing
A beauty in discos
N ice and caring
C ute, loving and cares about her dancing
I n the swing she is the dancing queen
N eat hair done gorgeously
G lamorous and decorated with clothes.

Natalie Hiddleston (9)
Drongan Primary School, Ayr

THE GLASS GHOST

G lass ghosts are made from glass
L iving under a glass cave
A man called King Glass Ghost is the king
S ome men like queens best
S ome men like kings best

G hosts hunt the night
H elp a glass ghost
O h no, a ghost
S tampede with ghosts
T he king is coming.

John Campbell (9)
Drongan Primary School, Ayr

SNOWING

One wee night
it was snowing
One night I couldn't
get to sleep
because the hailstones
were hitting on the window.
I had a dream about a snowman
out in the garden,
in the snow playing.

Vicky McDonald (9)
Drongan Primary School, Ayr

My Room

In my room I watch TV.
Sometimes it's a complete mess.
In my room I play the PlayStation.
In my room I use my imagination.
In my room I play board games.

In my room I fight with my brother.
In my room I go to sleep.
In my bed I have lots of teddies.
In my room I watch my brother act.
In my room I can stay up late.

In my room I make my bed.
In my room I clap my pet.
In my room I get changed.
In my room I clean my floor.
In my room I do exercises.

James Fleming (11)
Drongan Primary School, Ayr

The Snowman

The snowman was white
With two black ears
And a red and blue tartan hat
He had a pipe
He had a tartan coat
He had his name on his coat
His name was Frosty the snowman.

Tracy Blackwell (9)
Drongan Primary School, Ayr

THE MONSTER TRIP

The monster sat on a mustard man
The mustard man said with tears in his eyes
'Pick on somebody your own size.'
The monster's in a muddle
He thinks he's a hot crossed bun.
And when he looks in a mirror
All he can see is five wee mice sitting in a row
Out comes something from the mirror,
It's a thick pink penguin.
He's got smelly feet, funny ears, pickles in his head
And last of all he's got really sharp teeth
The monster went on and on walking
Down the road. Ha! Ha! Ha!
He fell into a bucket of walking feet.
He got into a car *broom! Broom! Broom*!
Heard something coming, crash into the car.
The monster got out and the man got out of the car,
The man said, 'Ho, turn around.'
The monster turned round, the man fell.
Broom! Broom! Off went the monster
And he had a good monster trip!

Alexa Ferguson (9)
Drongan Primary School, Ayr

IN THE MORNING

In the morning of Monday all I want is a sleep.
In the morning of Monday I only take one peep.
In the morning of Monday 'Get up' is all my parents say.
In the morning of Monday I stay in my bed.

In the mornings of summer I get straight up.
In the mornings of summer I walk the neighbour's pup.
In the mornings of summer I want to go to the sea.
In the mornings of summer I watch TV.

In the mornings of weekends I stay in my bed.
In the mornings of weekends I make toast with bread.
In the mornings of weekends I'm glad there's no school.
In the mornings of weekends it is really cool.

In the mornings of winter I lie there cold.
In the mornings of winter 'Get up' I am told.
In the mornings of winter I'm frozen to the spot.
In the mornings of winter I wish it was warm a lot!

Duncan Lucy (11)
Drongan Primary School, Ayr

THE SNOWFLAKE

One night I went to my bed
And I woke up, I heard a bang.
And there was a bigger bang
Than the last time.

And then I looked out,
It was hailstones.
One bang went off and then they stopped.

Jamie Main (9)
Drongan Primary School, Ayr

MY FANTASY LAND

In my dreams I go to a fantasy land
Where the houses are purple and silver.
Everybody there is happy
They are never sad.

I play games with the little children
And I go and visit the King.
I pick apples off the trees
And go riding on white horses with purple manes.

I like to do fun things
When I'm there.
I paint pictures and play games
I sing songs with the little princesses.

I visit the baker and buy cakes
For the little children
I like this fantasy land
It is called Wonderland.

Paula Greig (10)
Drongan Primary School, Ayr

THE SCOTLAND PEOPLE

They wear tartan kilts and eat haggis.
They do long jumps and play the bagpipes.
They have heavy shoes and stinky breath.
Have you guessed yet?
Some have long hair and some have beards.
Orange, black, grey, yellow, brown.
Have you guessed? . . . It's the Highland Scotsmen.
Strong guys, cool hair, big muscles, the Highlanders.

Megan Rae (9)
Drongan Primary School, Ayr

SUNNY DAYS

On sunny days
I like to go out to play
We run about and shout and say
'What a very lovely sunny day.'

When it's time for tea
We don't all jump with glee
But sometimes we go to the sea
And that is all about me.

I like to have picnics
And run about with sticks
Then I will be sick
Because of all the sweets.

I like to have little treats
Then I play hide and seek
And I have a little peek
Then they all say that I cheat.

Then I say that I'm not seeking
Because you're saying that I'm cheating
So we have a little meeting
And then I say, 'No more cheating.'

Kerri Ralph (11)
Drongan Primary School, Ayr

MY FANTASY LAND

My fantasy land is great fun
Everybody is having lots of fun
My fantasy land is a theme park
More like a roller coaster park
There is a roller coaster called the Bullet
It goes at the speed of a bullet.

There is a water splash called Canoc Creek
When you move, it begins to creak
There are go-karts there
At the queue, everybody's there.

My fantasy land has a swimming pool
You can play volleyball in the pool
There is a slide
It is very wide.

My fantasy land has a football park
My fantasy has animals
There are also some mammals.
At my fantasy land there is a horror land
Everybody screams going through it.

Mark McCubbin (11)
Drongan Primary School, Ayr

ALIEN PLANET

The alien planet is very scary
There are hundreds of monsters there
They have four legs, five eyes,
Blue body and six arms
That's what's on the alien planet.

The alien planet is very spooky
They have humans as pets
They have cars that hover
The cars just look like our pets
That's what's on the alien planet.

The alien planet is very large
They have hundreds of rainstorms
But it is not rainwater, it is meteors
They have houses made of stone
But the houses are underground
That's what's on the alien planet.

The alien planet is very weird
They eat worms, snails and slugs
That's what they call food
The alien planet is very disgusting
That's what's on the alien planet.

James Truesdale (11)
Drongan Primary School, Ayr

MY ROOM

In my room it is so much fun.
In my room it is lots of fun to run.
And my room is mostly a tip
So I have to tidy it.
Every time I tidy it, it's very, very tidy.

My friends come over to stay in my room
And all my friends like to stay in my room
They like it because I have lots of toys
Not one of my friends don't like my toys.

All my friends think my room is the best
But I don't think my room is the best
My room is big and very, very wide
And quite long, like a slide.

Every Saturday all my friends want to stay
Last Saturday I picked my friend Paul to stay
He liked to stay the night in my room
I liked him to stay in my tidy room.

My friend Paul said it's the biggest room he has been in
But it is certainly not the biggest room I've been in
In my room I have this electric toy that moves
My best friend John likes it when that toy moves.

Andrew Brown (10)
Drongan Primary School, Ayr

DANCING

Monday night for dancing.
First day of the week.
Getting my costume on
And dancing shoes on my feet.

Monday night for dancing.
Practice my routine.
My fancy feet are dancing.
Remember to practice for the team.

Monday night for dancing.
Out into the car.
Driving along the road.
It isn't very far.

Monday night for dancing.
Get dropped off just in time.
Go down the corridor.
Yes! We got there just fine.

Monday night for dancing.
We are ready and raring to go.
I'm going to do my routine.
Do you think I'll steal the show?

Laura Jess (11)
Drongan Primary School, Ayr

MY FRIENDS

My friends are always kind to me.
I would never let them down.
We've played together since nursery school
And we will never forget that.

We've had a bit of falling out
But we always make back up.
I'll never forget the time
When we dressed up as Sandy and Danny out of Grease

We like to go to the town and we like going swimming.
We like dancing and doing all sorts of stuff
But most of all we like singing.

I met my friend on holiday
In the most exciting place, Florida.
We went to a theme park and went on all the rides.
We mostly liked the one that went upside down.

I hope we'll be friends forever
Until we are old
But I'll never forget my best friends.

Nicole Forrest (11)
Drongan Primary School, Ayr

SNOW DAY

S now is fun to play with.
N ow when it is snowy you came make a snowman.
O n a snowy day it is cold.
W hen it is a snowy day you can have a snowball fight.

D ay is when you can play.
A nd when it is a snowy day you have fun.
Y es I said when it is a snowy day you can make a snowman.

Belinda Graham (9)
Drongan Primary School, Ayr

MY SPECIAL WORLD

S pringtime is when nature starts a new life.
P icnics on the beach, a lot of fun with food and drink.
E njoyment, laughter and friendship, it will always last.
C orn, carrots, vegetables and fruit, without them we
                              would not be healthy.
I f we had not had transport we could not go far so we are lucky.
A nimals are a big part of our world, for nature and pets for fun.
L ife is in us all, we need it to think and move.

W ho made the world? No one knows, who cares? We should
                              respect it all.
O n earth, in space, there is a sun. It is warm and beautiful to look at.
R ock is hard, spiky, smooth and heavy. You sometimes throw them.
L ots of people live in this planet, so it is special.
D on't pollute this world. It is fine the way it is!

Phillip Stewart (10)
Dunoon Primary School, Dunoon

LOYALTY IS...

Loyalty is . . . fighting for freedom, whatever it takes.
Loyalty is . . . family that should always come first.
Loyalty is . . . friends that should always come first.
Loyalty is . . . a pet that should be there to talk to you when you
                                                               are lonely.
Loyalty is . . . someone that will be willing to give up their life
                                               for what they believe in.
Loyalty is . . . hobbies which give you something to do in
                                               your spare time.
Loyalty is . . . helping out in all ways possible.
Loyalty is . . . serving your Queen as much as you can.
Loyalty is . . . sticking by your friend whatever happens.
Loyalty is . . . helping to make your country better and safe.
Loyalty is . . . hope which you should never give up on.
Loyalty is . . . looking after my niece who is only a year old.
Loyalty is . . . going to school and doing your best.
Loyalty, loyalty, that is what loyalty is all about.

Angela Kirkwood (10)
Dunoon Primary School, Dunoon

SPACE

S   tars are gliding through the night, watch them,
                                 watch them shine so bright.
P   luto is the smallest planet, colder than its moon,
       but I think Pluto is the nicest and it will be cuter than me soon
A   liens roam all over the galaxy, eating everything in sight
          but if you take it a bit slower you'll get there by night.
C   omets sneak across the galaxy, swishing there and back.
        They're going too fast. I can't see them! Watch out, don't crash.
E   arth is warmer and cuddlier than others. So I've decided
          to go back. I've had my day in space, so that's that.

Isla Davidson (8)
Dunoon Primary School, Dunoon

THE MAN WHO WENT TO THE MOON

In
1995 there
was a man who
went to the moon
it was a funny sight because
when it was day
he thought it was night and
one day he thought
it was night
but it was day
and he feel asleep at
daytime and the rocket
went *booooooooooooooooooooo*
ooooooommmmmmmmmm
because an asteroid
hit it and it looked like
fireworks!

***James Campbell** (8)*
Dunoon Primary School, Dunoon

SPACE DEBRIS

S   un is shining every day.
P   luto is the farthest away.
A   stronauts walk very, very slow.
C   omets are the best, they glow.
E   arth is my best planet, I would not like it to go.

***Jack Cleugh** (8)*
Dunoon Primary School, Dunoon

A STORMY NIGHT

The sky is dark, a storm is near,
All is quiet, something to fear,
A low rumbling noise can be heard,
Children are hiding, something to dread.

The sky is exploding, a crashing sound,
As lightning flashes all around,
Dogs are barking, babies cry,
As this terrifying noise fills the sky.

Thundering clouds pour out the rain,
Soon everything will be fresh again,
Rushing wind and swaying trees,
It's much more than a summer's breeze.

Almost as quickly as it had begun,
The clouds part and out pops the sun,
All is calm, all is bright,
But we'll never forget that stormy night.

Karen Mackay (11)
Dunoon Primary School, Dunoon

SPACE

S   un is hot.
P   lanets are shapes.
A   liens are landing.
C   omets are flying.
E   arth is floating.

Iain Johnstone (8)
Dunoon Primary School, Dunoon

THE WITCH

There was an old witch
That lived far away
It wasn't very often she had something to say.

The witch was as crooked as a stick
And she just sat there and started to pick.
Horrible teeth that she tried to hide
She didn't really have much pride.

The witch just sat there all alone,
Sometimes she wondered if she could buy a phone.
Don't think she could do that, not enough money
She would rather just sit there and suck on honey.

Mad as a hatter she could be.
Sometimes she would sit all day in a tree.
No one to love her, no one to care,
She would just sit all day and stare.

Lucky this is a story,
And not true life.
Unless this old lady
Is somebody's wife?

Lyndsay Derrett (11)
Dunoon Primary School, Dunoon

SPACE

S   un and moon so yellow and bright.
P   lanets so small you can hardly see them.
A   steroids belt and Uranus' ring.
C   omets so fiery you can see them.
E   arth is my home and I love it.

Eilidh Goslan (8)
Dunoon Primary School, Dunoon

SPACE

If I go up to space
I can see Mars
If I go up higher
I can see the stars
I would think I was so
Far up from Earth that I
Would lose something and
Then I would
Search
Then I would see Pluto,
The last one from the sun
But I can't go too close
Or I might freeze
I might see Mercury
A tiny little planet and
I might see Janet
On a planet.

Angela Phillips (8)
Dunoon Primary School, Dunoon

SPACE ADVENTURE

Some of the planets are often cold
Like Pluto and Neptune
All the rest are hotter
Rings around Saturn are sparkly
But yet all planets are still there
I think they are terrific
I live on Earth
It is the best planet ever
My trip to the moon
Won't happen for a long time yet!

Claire Clark (8)
Dunoon Primary School, Dunoon

MANDY BROWN

Mandy Brown had a huge frown,
And spent her life looking down.
She was tall and thin with greasy hair
Probably because no one gave her tender loving care.

She lived in a house that was dirty and damp
And her next door neighbour was a smelly old tramp.
She slept in a sack on her kitchen floor,
Cold, lonely and very sore.

She had a mum who didn't care,
About her clothes and messy hair.
Her mum took drugs very well,
To try and escape this living hell.

Mandy went to school every morning
And never took the teacher's warning.
The teacher said, 'Get out of Class!
I'll deal with you later, you bad lass!'

Mandy's life was full of woe,
Until she found her father Joe.
He turned her life all around
And now no happier girl can be found.

Katie Thomson (11)
Dunoon Primary School, Dunoon

A Hallowe'en Spell

Cauldron bubble
Fire burn
Sting of bee
And gran's knobbly knee

Eye of human
Tooth of dog
And one big fat slimy frog

Mix together
Blend in well
Make a humungous smell

Exploding potion
Will burn in your face
Can be smelt in outer space.

Allan Robson (12)
Dunoon Primary School, Dunoon

Space

S   un is our star, it is a big ball of gas.
                       It is so hot it could burn grass.
P   lanets are where things live. I live on earth and
                                I've been to Perth.
A   steroids are rocks. But I eat lollipops.
C   omets and cats are things I don't like.
E   arth to Mars is what I say to my brother
                                When he is not listening.

Heather Morton (8)
Dunoon Primary School, Dunoon

GEOFFREY GRAY

Geoffrey Gray walks through the town,
With the biggest and saddest ever frown,
He listens to the people laughing and talking,
Whilst he keeps on walking and walking.

His hair sticks out all over the place
And there's mud covering his thin, pale face
His body is as skinny as a stick,
While other children are as solid as a brick.

For dinner he searches through the bins,
And peeks at people eating at cafes and inns.
Not for him, a hot three course meal,
More like a crust of bread and orange peel.

Deep in his heart, under his frown,
He wants to be part of the people in the town.
Sitting on a bench, watching the world go by,
He gives the most deepest, solemn sigh.

Neil McClelland (11)
Dunoon Primary School, Dunoon

MY SPACE RIDE

S   tars tell stories like, for instance, Orion.
P   luto is the furthest away. This day has to be remembered.
A   steroids fly through space. They are the best because they glow.
C   ome with me, I cannot see without you.
E   arth is a warm planet. I have got used to it now. I must go.
       I have had my day in space but Earth is the one for me.

Fraser Davidson (8)
Dunoon Primary School, Dunoon

SPACE POEM

There is nothing to comfort you,
Not even a drop of air,
As you wander along in the middle of nowhere,
Until you reach the moon,
Look down, and you see home,
Look up, and you see . . . *magic!*

Paige Walker (9)
Dunoon Primary School, Dunoon

IN SPACE

Stars twinkle in space
With Venus and his angry face,
Orion's belt and his sword
Pointing to his faithful dog.
Jupiter and his big red scar
Scaring every lonely star
Satellites orbit the universe
While we are here on planet Earth.

Ryan Bogan (9)
Dunoon Primary School, Dunoon

SPACE

S pace is full of galaxies
P lanets and stars
A planet small and red called Mars
C old planet called Pluto all alone
E arth is the planet we call home.

Lauren Cowan (9)
Dunoon Primary School, Dunoon

SPACE

Orion's belt is in the west
With his dog looking its best
The milky way is in the sky too
Who knows what it's supposed to do?
Seven sisters in a line
All the planets looking fine
So say goodnight to the sky
Soon it will be morning bye and bye.

Katie Fletcher (9)
Dunoon Primary School, Dunoon

A SPACE POEM

Meteorites silently rolling through space
Past the milky way and Orion at a really slow pace.
Lots of planets for us to see
Venus, Earth, Pluto and Mercury
And there are more planets that like to turn
Jupiter, Uranus, Neptune, Mars and Saturn.

Aidan Steel (9)
Dunoon Primary School, Dunoon

SPACE

Space is big with lots of room
Pluto, Earth and Mars
A wounded planet, that brave Jupiter
Cold and lonely in outer space
Guarded by loyal Saturn.

Alisha McMillan (9)
Dunoon Primary School, Dunoon

WITCHES

Witches, witches crouching in ditches,
Waiting for girls and boys,
They wait there all day and during the night,
Waiting to give a poor soul a fright!

The witches are warty, smelly too,
They sit there all day making a potion or two,
Their names are Meg, Morag and Mary,
Their noses are long and their chins are hairy!

They live far, in the middle of a wood,
No one goes near and nobody should,
People have gone to visit their den,
These people have never been seen again!

Hannah Gray (10)
Dunoon Primary School, Dunoon

SPACE

Listen to the sound,
The sound of space.
Taste the milky way,
Enjoy the flavour of Mars.
Look at the precious planets,
The moon, the stars and sun.
They're all having fun.
Smell that special space,
Feel that special place.

Leah Campbell (9)
Dunoon Primary School, Dunoon

CHRISTMAS DAY

C is for colours that shine in the night,
H is for homes with their lovely lights,
R is for Richard who loves the presents,
I is for the ice that slips up the pheasants,
S is for Santa who says, 'Ho ho ho,'
T is for Tommy who plays in the snow,
M is for mistletoe where people kiss,
A is for 'A very Merry Christmas!'
S is for stable where Jesus was born,

D is for Dancer who always feels warm,
A is for a present to open,
Y is for you, caring and hoping.

Richard A Shea (11)
Dunoon Primary School, Dunoon

MY MAGIC SPELL

Eye of newt, skeleton's skull,
Toe from foot, part of gull,
Smelly socks, wing of bat,
An old fox, fur from cat,
Blood from dog, slugs and snails,
Hop from frog, puppy dog tails,
Two owl wings, elephants' brains,
Double, double, toil and trouble,
Fire burn and cauldron bubbles,
This is the end of our immortal spell,
Hope this makes you all unwell.

Laura Stewart (10)
Dunoon Primary School, Dunoon

SARAH RED

There once was a girl called Sarah Red,
Who was very poor and badly fed,
She never, ever came to school,
But mucked around, playing the fool.

Now this wee girl called Sarah Red,
Who had blonde hair upon her head,
Had eyes of brilliant sapphire blue,
And a mouth that always smiled at you.

The clothes belonging to Sarah Red,
Were not brand new, but old instead,
The shoes she wore upon her feet,
Had little holes, although discreet.

So who abandoned Sarah Red?
A man who drank too much they said,
And so poor Sarah tried to cope,
Her mum had died, there seemed no hope.

Then what became of Sarah Red?
With the golden hair upon her head,
A neighbour said, 'Please come with me,
You too can join my family!'

So all ended well for Sarah Red,
She even slept upon a bed!
She got new clothes, shoes for her feet,
Her life, at last, it was complete.

Shona Hamlet (11)
Dunoon Primary School, Dunoon

MILLIE BROWN

Millie Brown comes to school with a frown,
Because her life has been turned around.
It was an awful day when her mother came to say.
'Your father was trapped in the mines today.'

With her long blonde hair all over the place,
And her beauty hidden by the dirt on her face.
Full of sorrow and little to eat,
She walks along slowly in her bare feet.

Her classroom today is sullen and sad,
For Millie is not the only one missing her dad.
They all sit in silence with nothing to say,
When their teacher Miss Brogan asks them to pray.

A loud siren screams through the village of Dundavers,
And the children rush out to find the fate of their fathers.
As the children rush down to the bottom of the stair,
Millie cries out, 'Let my father be there.'

After eighteen hours staring death in the face,
The miners emerge at a slow pace.
Millie watched from the foot of the hill,
As a familiar figure stood perfectly still.

While screaming aloud, she ran through the crowd,
Outstretched arms to meet her.
Being so poor did not matter anymore,
As a loving father did greet her.

Samantha Campbell (11)
Dunoon Primary School, Dunoon

MY GRANDPARENTS

I'm sure my granny is a witch,
Her broomstick gives it away,
Her pointed hat as black as pitch,
And her cat keeps going astray!

My grandpa is a warlock,
He turned into a toad,
And all the letters he writes to me,
Are always in Morse code!

They both live in the dungeon,
The one with lots of cells,
And there in the dark, at the dead of night,
Is where they cast their spells.

My gran gets up at midnight,
To dance around the lawn,
She brings round all her cronies,
And they go away at dawn!

My grandpa hops to the pond,
To meet his nightly friends,
All of them are warlock toads,
And they all have separate dens!

My grandparents like Earl Grey tea,
They sip the day away!
And I think they're taking, lucky me,
On a broomstick ride, tonight!

Meghan Clark (10)
Dunoon Primary School, Dunoon

CHARLOTTE BROWN

Charlotte Brown wears a frown,
Her smile is always upside down,
Her big blue eyes are full of tears,
Since her father disappeared.

Her mother is as poor as a little white mouse,
And has barely enough to afford a house,
Grandma Brown lives quite near,
But never, ever wants to hear.

Charlotte Brown is very shy,
And all her teachers wonder why,
After school she hobbles along,
Trying to sing a happy song.

PC Mackay came round one day,
To take poor Charlotte Brown away,
After that Charlotte cried,
Because her mother had sadly died.

Charlotte Brown wears a frown,
Her smile is always upside down,
Perhaps one day her life will change,
To Charlotte Brown it would be very strange.

Mhairi Cameron (11)
Dunoon Primary School, Dunoon

ME!

Into this world I came to see,
What Jesus Christ had given me.
My fingers, my hands, my feet, my nose,
And even all my tiny toes.

He gave me a nose so I can smell,
And he gave me my blue sapphire eyes as well.
He gave me two ears at the side of my head,
And gave me a mouth so I can be fed.

He gave me a body to wriggle and walk,
And gave me a mouth so that I can talk.
He gave me some hair that I can brush,
And gave me some legs if I was in a rush.

Now you can see how he made me,
To roam, to walk and to be free.
Now you can see that is the way he made me!

Jenna Cushley (11)
Dunoon Primary School, Dunoon

MY SPELL . . . (HALLOWE'EN)

Ears of rats, tails of cats.
Giant feet, bits of wheat.
Bats' wings, bee stings.
Human skull and one football.
One big smile which will take a while.
This is the end of my witches' spell.

Michelle Campbell (10)
Dunoon Primary School, Dunoon

COUNTING THROUGH THE CALENDAR

January turns a brand new page,
Starts the year of a brand new age,
February brings the rainy cloud's dew,
And the romantic Valentine's Day too.

March brings the wet season of spring,
Young ones, the whole world will bring,
April's pretty flowers bloom with pride,
While in the Easter Bunny's sack, chocolate eggs ride.

May's the month when the warmth arrives,
Busy bees buzz out of their hives,
June means time for fun on the beach,
The next half of the year is nearly in reach.

July has holidays, activities and sports,
Rock climbing and competing in tennis courts,
It's August, time to go back to school,
The last month of summer, still trying to keep cool.

September brings autumn's wind and leaves,
Reds and golds fall off the trees,
October, pumpkins, witches and ghosts,
Treats they want and tricks they boast.

November's month starts off with a bang,
Colourful sparks split out of their gang.
The festive Christmas arrives in December,
What a wonderful year it is to remember!

Garry Baird (11)
Dunoon Primary School, Dunoon

RACISM

Racism, racism fills the town,
The abused people's faces can only frown,
Laughing and mocking, the people are,
Little do they know that person could become a star.

The depressed person longs for a day,
A day when those people can laugh and play,
Where everyone can live in perfect happiness,
Free from prejudice, bigotry and nastiness.

The troubled person wishes to be an actor,
And wear fancy make-up, made by Max Factor,
The person is denied because of their skin,
It's not what's outside that matters, it's what's in.

The person says to herself, 'This is not fair,'
Those people are nasty, they really don't care,
Who they hurt for their amusement,
I am upset; I have come to this conclusion.

I will go to court and fight for the right
To help get out of this horrible plight,
This will be a new world order,
To be treated equally, across every border.

Now everyone is treated the same,
The people who made fun are now in shame,
Laughing and joking all together,
This rule will stand forever and ever.

James Tato (11)
Dunoon Primary School, Dunoon

CHRISTMAS DAY

When all the boys and girls are asleep,
Santa comes down the chimney, creep, creep, creep.
He puts all the presents under the tree.
And when the boys and girls wake up
They shout 'Yippee! Yippee!'

He goes to the other towns, cities too!
To make other children happy as me and you.
But when he leaves, children cry tears.
But don't worry, Santa will be back next year.

It's that time of year and Santa came back
With all the presents in his sack.
The children are sleeping in their bed
Quietly resting their little heads.

When the children's alarm clock
Goes off at seven in the morning.
They are loud and they wake up their parents
And they don't get a warning.
The children get up without a yawn
And when their parents go downstairs,
Their presents are gone!

The Christmas wrapping paper is all over the floor
And mum and dad need to sweep it out of the door.
Christmas is over and the children are sad
But it's ok, it's not that bad!

Michael McArthur (11)
Dunoon Primary School, Dunoon

CHRISTMAS IS . . .

Christmas is . . . for loving and giving and of course receiving.
Christmas is . . . the time you spend with all the family.
Christmas is . . . when children's laughter spreads all around the town.
Christmas is . . . a celebration with many decorations.
Christmas is . . . when a special someone goes under the mistletoe.
Christmas is . . . when sleigh bells ring and carols sing.
Christmas is . . . when doors open with chocolate inside.
Christmas is . . . filled up stockings above the fire.
Christmas is . . . snuggling up in bed while opening many small
                                                      but fun presents.
Christmas is . . . around a huge table with foods of all different kinds.
Christmas is . . . when twinkling stars shine above the house so bright.
Christmas is . . . when children's and adults' faces light up with joy.
Christmas is . . . a tree lit up with homemade treasures all around
                                                      and near.
Christmas is . . . when someone comes so silently and sneaks a
                                                      present or two.
Christmas is . . . white snowmen with button mouths and carrot noses.
Christmas is . . . a day which will stay with you forever.

Megan Flaherty (9)
Dunoon Primary School, Dunoon

SPACE

S   hooting stars crossing the dark sky
P   lanets are moving and swirling.
A   liens doing the moonwalk dance
C   old or hot, day and night
E   njoying staring at the stars, shining down on Earth.

Jennifer Finlayson (9)
Dunoon Primary School, Dunoon

LOYALTY IS ...

Loyalty is helping people when they need helping.
Loyalty is keeping a deep, dark secret from others.
Loyalty is looking after my cousins at any time.
Loyalty is keeping your promises and not breaking them.
Loyalty is sticking up for family and friends when they are in trouble.
Loyalty is when I help my budgie to learn to play with his toys better.
Loyalty is when I feed my fish and try to make him more
                                      confident when I am at his tank.
Loyalty is when I help my gran and grandpa do things
                                            around the house.
Loyalty is caring for others and not just yourself.
Loyalty is giving money to charity or giving away old toys and
                                      clothes to people in poorer places.
Loyalty is being truthful about things that you have done.
Loyalty is never falling out with your friends.

Nikki Goffin (10)
Dunoon Primary School, Dunoon

SPACE

Jupiter is big, Pluto is small,
Saturn's rocky ring surrounds it all.
If you have seen the moon's sea,
You'll agree that it is called tranquillity.
Then soon it will get black and dark,
Will Orion's dog begin to bark?

Scott Johnstone (9)
Dunoon Primary School, Dunoon

CHRISTMAS

A
Star twinkling,
Big fat turkeys
Cracking till cooked,
Trees swaying in the
Soft, cold breeze,
Carol singing in the
Freezing cold,
Bright lights shining in
The foggy mist,
Snow melting, crackling
From the sunlight,
Turkey cooking through
And through.
Mince pies sizzling
Present ripping open
Jesus wailing in a manger,
Trumpets blaring louder
And louder.
Angels singing softly
And tenderly.
At home, giggling
Laughter fills the
Room.

Gillian Downie (10)
Dunoon Primary School, Dunoon

CHRISTMAS

A
Star
Shimmering
Angels praising
Shepherds kneeling
Santa's coming
Gifts receiving
Children thanking
Turkeys roasting
Potatoes bubbling
Water boiling
People eating
Champagne drinking
Cracker pulling
Parents laughing
Kids sledging
On snow sparkling
Bells jingling
Tree decorating
Snowman building
Snowball throwing
Chocolate eating
No schooling
Lights glittering
Tinsel swaying
Icicles dripping
Everyone is partying
Partying and dancing
Why? Christmas is coming.

Hannah MacPherson (10)
Dunoon Primary School, Dunoon

CHRISTMAS IS . . .

Christmas is . . . pretty when it snows.
Christmas is . . . fun to put up the tree.
Christmas is . . . great fun to open the presents.
Christmas is . . . to spend time with your family.
Christmas is . . . a very joyful holiday.
Christmas is . . . a time for sharing.
Christmas is . . . a time when you get good dinner
Christmas is . . . a time when Santa comes.
Christmas is . . . a time to go sledging.
Christmas is . . . a time to have a snowball fight.
Christmas is . . . a time to build a snowman.
Christmas is . . . about giving and receiving.
Christmas is . . . a time to enjoy yourself.
Christmas is . . . a time to have fun.
Christmas is . . . a time to have fun with your family.
Christmas is . . . great when you get to eat the pudding.
Christmas is . . . a time for caring.
Christmas is . . . a time for play.
Christmas is . . . a time when your stockings go up.
Christmas is . . . a day of joy.
Christmas is . . . a time to realise what you have.

Hazel Galloway (10)
Dunoon Primary School, Dunoon

SPACE

The sun is shining every day.
Neptune is far away.
And all the aliens cannot say.
That your rocket is in the way.

Cian Bennett (8)
Dunoon Primary School, Dunoon

LOYALTY

Loyalty is taking care of animals.
Loyalty is playing with your friends when they're lonely.
Loyalty is having a true friendship.
Loyalty is helping people in need.
Loyalty is never abusing pets or children.
Loyalty is not doing graffiti.
Loyalty is sticking up for your brothers, sisters and friends.
Loyalty is helping the Red Cross.
Loyalty is keeping secrets that you've been told.
Loyalty is helping your family.
Loyalty is making a true friendship last.
Loyalty is bravery
Loyalty is having faith in yourself.
Loyalty is happiness and freedom.
Loyalty is being a true friend.
Loyalty is sticking together as a group.
Loyalty is caring for each other.
Loyalty is respecting what people do for you.
Loyalty is giving money to charity.
Loyalty is helping people even though they made you feel down.
Loyalty is caring for your pets.
Loyalty is helping your parents, even if they shout at you.
Loyalty is helping the elderly.
Loyalty is helping your brother or sister, even if they hit you.
Loyalty is to not be jealous.
Loyalty is people that aren't greedy.
Loyalty is having a family that cares.
Loyalty is being there for one another.
Loyalty is helping, caring, being there for each other
                       and helping people, even animals.

Katriona Maclean (10)
Dunoon Primary School, Dunoon

LOYALTY

Loyalty is helping a friend in need.
Loyalty is sticking to your words.
Loyalty is helping others younger than you.
Loyalty is teaching the P1s about school.
Loyalty is helping my niece who is one and my nephew who is three.
Loyalty is keeping your friends' secrets.
Loyalty is helping the elderly with their shopping.
Loyalty is never abusing pets.
Loyalty is never calling friends names.
Loyalty is never leaving anyone out.
Loyalty is helping people through hard times.
Loyalty is trying not to fight with your brothers or sisters.
Loyalty is going on errands for family who need it.
Loyalty is being mature about friends' problems.
Loyalty is never giving up.
Loyalty is helping new people settle in.
Loyalty is taking your brothers and sisters out to play when
                      your mum and dad need some sleep.
Loyalty is never leaving a friend alone to go and play with
                                    someone else.
Loyalty is trying to be friends with everyone.
Loyalty is always telling the truth and never blaming someone else.
Loyalty is never starting wars.
Loyalty is being true to your country.
Loyalty is giving money to charities.
Loyalty is sticking up for family and friends.

Leanne Frace (10)
Dunoon Primary School, Dunoon

LOYALTY IS...

Loyalty is . . . a loving heart and a friendly soul.
Loyalty is . . . a willing and helpful attitude.
Loyalty is . . . a caring concern.
Loyalty is . . . forever fighting for freedom.
Loyalty is . . . being there for friends and family.
Loyalty is . . . a trustworthy friend.
Loyalty is . . . helping our environment.
Loyalty is . . . not to bully.
Loyalty is . . . respecting other people.
Loyalty is . . . a kind response to those who believe in you.
Loyalty is . . . standing up, no matter what others think of you.
Loyalty is . . . sticking with friends no matter what.
Loyalty is . . . helping charities raise money.
Loyalty is . . . listening to other people's ideas.
Loyalty is . . . devotion to your pets.

Morgan Elliott (10)
Dunoon Primary School, Dunoon

NOVEMBER

No sun
No fun
No snow quite yet
No people I've met
No playing outside
No birds out
No flowers
No snow showers
No calm weather
No bird feathers
November!

Shannon Hanson (10)
Duror Primary School, Appin

SUMMER!

No snow
No snowmen
No Santa
No presents
No cold
No strong winds
No wild winds
No gloves
No scarves
No heavy jackets
No sitting by the fire
No bowls of soup
No slipping and sliding
It's summertime!

Jack Moffit (8)
Duror Primary School, Appin

FROST IN THE COUNTRY

Dark and cold with it.
Silent and chill with it.
Every star like a diamond sparkling.
Every minute the sky is darkening.
Some trees have long black branches glistening.
And all the small dark creatures are listening
Under your feet it is very cold.
And the frozen leaves have turned into mould.

Hannah Malcolm (10)
Duror Primary School, Appin

FROST IN THE COUNTRY

The wind fanned
on the winter wonderland,
The trees were bare
In the cold night air,
The branches were glistening
Whilst the wind was whistling,
The grass was bound in it,
The wonderland had no sound in it,
A void of stars,
No sound of any car

The mouse was lost
In the midnight frost,
It skated on
The icy pond,
A cat came over to it
Where the pond was moonlit,
A feline pounce and the mouse was dead,
It sank below the ice like lead.

Ben Moffit, Jessie Blanchard & Claire Chrystal (10)
Duror Primary School, Appin

THE HEADLESS HORSEMAN

The road is a silver stream
The wind is a current of water
The moon is a bright, glowing marble
He is skulking behind a tree
The headless horseman is waiting
Just waiting to get you and me.

Carol Salmon (10)
Duror Primary School, Appin

HAYLEY

Hayley is my friend,
She plays with me all day.
She will play with me in a funny way.
We go outside and have some fun.
She puts snow down my back.
She has very, very smelly feet.
I think that she is a clown.
But she thinks I'm one too.

Leah Tetstall (9)
Fallin Primary School, Fallin

KAITLYN

K aitlyn is kind and funny.
A lways telling jokes.
I miss her so much, because she left.
T alking about good things all the time.
L ively.
Y oung.
N ever doing anything wrong.

Louise Boyle (9)
Fallin Primary School, Fallin

CHRISY

Oh Chrisy, oh Chrisy, you are so mean, but not so keen.
So you'd better get that grumpy mood out of your heard before bed
Or no present from Santa again. Ok Chrisy?
No, I won't get that grumpy mood out of my head.
Fine then you'll just get a row.

Aaron Hazel (9)
Fallin Primary School, Fallin

My Home

In the morning my house is very warm
But cold outside.
In the morning I get ready
For school every day, except the weekend.
When I come from school
I watch TV.

At night my house
Is very cold, even outside.
At night I have my supper, which is usually
Toast and cheese then
I go to bed
And sleep the night
Away.

Kevin Cochrane (9)
Fallin Primary School, Fallin

Misty My Gran's Dog

M is for mighty like the strength of a husky.
I is for independence, that is her middle name.
S is for splendid, Misty is such a splendid dog.
T is for terrific, she is such a terrific swimmer.
Y is for younger, she is much younger than me, but not in
                                          doggy years.

Abbie Rixon (9)
Fallin Primary School, Fallin

GOING ON HOLIDAY

I love the swimming pool and the sun.
I love going on planes.
I like sun bathing.
I like splashing water about.
I like going on boats on my holidays, and I like fishing on my holidays.
I like going out on my holidays at night.
I like going out at night and buying things on my holidays.
I like jumping in the pool and playing snooker.
I like drinking shandy on my holidays
I love going up hills.
I hate wearing hats and sandals too.

Johnny Hunter (9)
Fallin Primary School, Fallin

SASHA

My gran's dog Sasha is very fast
Just those little feet running past
She is very brave
Like the Greyfriars Bobby sitting on his grave
Show her a biscuit and she runs like a whippet
She is smart and strong
But sometimes she feels like crawling into a cave
She will playfully bite
Until I start a fight
She is the best dog in the world
And I love her.

Boab Thomson (9)
Fallin Primary School, Fallin

MY FRIENDS

M y friends are always there for me.
Y oung and intelligent they are.

F unny, caring and daring.
R adiant when we're together.
I ntelligent at languages.
E njoy each other's company.
N ever annoying.
D own to earth.
S pecial to me in every way.

Shauni McGregor (9)
Fallin Primary School, Fallin

A DAY OUT

On the sandy beach
I walked along
With a soft breeze
And the golden sand
I could hear the seagulls above
The sun was just going down
And you could see the reflection
Upon the water
Then
I walked home.

Shaun Blackwood (11)
Forehill Primary School, Ayr

QUIET BEACH

I wanted to go to the beach,
So my mum took me round,
I got out of the car
And what did I hear?
Not a squawk,
Not a squeak,
Not a sound.

The sand was soft and creeping,
Some sea creatures were peeping.
The waves were not lapping,
The sun was nearly napping.

There was hardly a sound,
On the calm, quiet beach.

Lisa Raftery (11)
Forehill Primary School, Ayr

THE SUMMERTIME BEACH

On the sandy beach, I strolled,
The warm sand pressing against my feet.
It is quiet.
The sky is cloudless.
The birds are soaring in the sky.
The brisk breeze brushing against my face.
On the horizon, a speedboat moves swiftly across the water.
At the edge of the water, the sea is lapping against the beach.
A sandcastle sits with a moat around the outer edge.
The sun makes the water evaporate.
That's what I call a beach!

Robert Walsh (11)
Forehill Primary School, Ayr

THE PUPPY DOG!

I am a little puppy dog
I like to run about
I have a friend called Molly
Who's pretty, without a doubt

She came to play the other day
We went running in the park
We skipped and jumped, had lots of fun
We played till it was dark

Along the road, we headed home
We waited at the door
I got my supper, a huge big bone
When I'd finished, I wanted more

Then the gate was open and Molly ran away
She barked as if to say
'I'll be back another day.'

Laura Williamson (11)
Forehill Primary School, Ayr

THE WINTER CALMNESS

The hibernating sand,
Rocks and mountains.

The seagulls squawking,
Flying and pecking.

The waves splashing,
Looping and wetting.

When all this is
A winter's day.

Grant Hoggitt (11)
Forehill Primary School, Ayr

THE WIND BLOWS

The wind blows,
The wind goes,
Bringing doon the rain,
The wind blows,
The wind goes,
On the nichts am hame alane

Hear the ghosties in the hall
Feart by bairns ane an' all
Let's no forget thae unco witches
Wi' faces green as fitba' pitches

The wind blows
The wind goes
Bringin' doon the rain
The wind blows
The wind goes
Am I safe here on my ain?

Wi' a click on goes the licht
A gentle fire in the nicht
Nae mair ghoulies in the hall
Nothing scary there at all

The wind blows
The wind goes
Bringin' doon the rain
The wind blows
The wind goes
On the nicht am hame alane.

Calum Brough (11)
Forehill Primary School, Ayr

SAME PLANET! DIFFERENT WORLD!

He looked out at the coloured cars
And all the restaurants, hotels and bars
I looked out at the cracked earth and sand
Not a dribble of water on the land

He scoffed chocolates, crisps and sweets
Buying himself lots of treats
I hunted for food with all my might
But there wasn't anything in sight

For drinks he had a wide selection
Cola and Tango are just some to mention
I only had what I could find
Of water this land is totally blind

At night he's tucked up warm and snug
With pillows, duvets and a furry rug
Me, I sleep on mud and dirt
My body no longer feels the hurt

His hectic life is full of work and play
There seems no end to his busy day
Me, I work from six till late
And just get enough money to put food on the plate

If you think he has got it all
All he's got is very small
I have two children and a wonderful wife
That's what gives me a perfect life.

Chloe Young (11)
Forehill Primary School, Ayr

HOMEWORK TIME!

Slop it on the table
Moan out loud
Lean on your elbow
Stare at the ground

Stare at the ceiling
Look up at the sky
It's a horrible feeling
Why, o' why?

I could easily debate
That it should be a crime
Oh how I hate
Homework time!

Stewart McLellan (11)
Forehill Primary School, Ayr

FRIENDS

Friends mean a lot to you and to me
What would we do without them?
No one to speak to
No one to turn to
No one to share your secrets with
Just you

Friends should stick by you
Right by your side
They shouldn't turn their back on you
Lead you astray
Or make you feel left out

Friends are your trustworthy companions through life.

Heather Carrington (11)
Forehill Primary School, Ayr

DAWN OF DUSK

As the great orange chieftain sets out of sight
In ride the black armies o' the night
And so the dawn a dusky war
The light ones canny win no more

And here begins an ending glow
As light sinks to the plains below
And our great chieftain now glows red
With blood that he has yet to shed

And with the light in their retreat
The darkness send out their last fleet
'Now darkness rules this world so small
The shadow shall pass over all!'

But lo! Bright soldier of light
Appears to save this evil night
Followed by a million more
Here to open light's great door

And so appears their greatest chief
Full of woe and full of grief
Half today, but full tomorrow
Then like a curved blade of sorrow

And so, for now, light defeats the black
Though darkness shouts, 'We will be back!'
And the great light chief comes from the west
Mastering his great light crest

Darkness flees into the east
Roaring like a wounded beast
'Though now of course light brings the day
Dark is never far away . . .'

Ruaraidh McPike (11)
Forehill Primary School, Ayr

MOTHER ROBIN

The buzzing of a bumble bee
An owl whooshing from tree to tree
The robin with its head up high
As high as a plane flying in the sky

Collecting for its family and no other
The robin does its duty as a mother
It spots a red, ripe berry growing near
While watching babies chirp and cheer

With the berry in its beak
And one large berry in its chest
It flies back to the nest
But the robin does not rest

For it spots a worm wiggling around
So silently and so sound
The robin sees its chance once more
And sweeps down to the forest floor

Triumphant again with its prize
Back again to the nest it flies
With swollen bellies the babies rest
And mother robin has done her best.

Ian Longworth (11)
Forehill Primary School, Ayr

THE DREAM KEEPER

When you lie in your bed at night
Trying to sleep with all your might
Think about the lonely dream keeper
In the cold, he's no sleeper!

He wanders through the lit up streets
While you dream about your sweets
He sends dreams in all sizes and shapes
One looked like a bunch of green grapes!

His face is as white as the clouds in the summer
His eyes couldn't have any more colour
His clothes are as ragged as they could be
He wears magic sandals that you cannot see

This magical thing is an amazing creature
Where does it come from, this fantastic feature?
Every good dream is caught and sent
By this amazing and wonderful gent!

When you lie in your bed at night
Trying to sleep with all your might
Think about the lonely dream keeper
In the cold at night, he's no sleeper!

Nicola Stirling (11)
Forehill Primary School, Ayr

THE FOUR SEASONS

Spring is growing flowers
And April showers
Babies riding in their prams
Fields of cuddly lambs

Summer is glorious sunshine
Holidays abroad all the time
Playing games on the beach
Loads of ice cream in flavours of peach

Autumn is bare trees
In and out of the branches goes a breeze
Hats and scarves to keep yourself warm
Because next month there will be quite a storm!

Winter is Christmas and snow
With presents under the tree, you couldn't say no
You'll want to try out your favourite present
If it's a bike, have a ride round your crescent!

Laura Alexander (11)
Forehill Primary School, Ayr

THE SOUND OF THE GLEN

Water trickling down the burn
The sky is lit up by the roaring sun
The air is fresh, the clouds are white
Not a person or sound heard or in sight

But I can hear a skylark's sweet song
It appears and sits on the post
After a while it flies over the hills
It is silent again, quiet and still.

Mairead McCrossan (11)
Forehill Primary School, Ayr

THE SANDY BEACH

There was once a lonely beach
The sand was soft
The water was wild
The air was free
That's all . . . ?
Sandy beach.

Melissa Hewitson (11)
Forehill Primary School, Ayr

HORRIBLE PEOPLE

'My name is . . .'
'What did you say?
I can't hear you.'
'Never mind.
Oh I got this yesterday.'
'What did you say?'
'Stop faking.'
I think it is sad
When people say things like that,
They must think they're deaf as a doorpost,
But once they learn it's not so nice
They'll already be doing it thrice.
'I went to such and such
On the summer holiday.'
'What?'
'Shut up.'
It must be upsetting
And embarrassing to be yelled at
All the time.
'Oh I got this on my birthday.'
'What?'

Aron Wright (9)
Kilchrenan Primary School, Taynuilt

ROLLER COASTER FUN

Yippee! Hullabaloo!
'Mum,' shouted a boy
'Can we go to a theme park too?'
'OK! Hurry up then
Get in!
Get in!
Buckle up!
Buckle up!'
Go! Go!
Go on a roller coaster
Get in! Get in!
Shouted a boy
'Come on, Mum.'

Emma Gillespie (8)
Kilchrenan Primary School, Taynuilt

FAMILY PETS

My gran's dog
She eats like a hog
My friend's cat
She's very, very fat
My sister's bird
She's totally absurd
My dad's dog
She really hates the fog
My mum's fish
She gave them to Aunt Trish
They are all the pets
That we took to the vet's.

Chloe Wilkie (9)
Kilchrenan Primary School, Taynuilt

THEME PARK FUN

People screaming
Running towards the theme park;
People going 'Yippee, yahoo!'
Running all over the place,
Space rides,
Spooky rides,
Bumper cars,
Roller coasters,
Masses,
Candyfloss,
Yum,
Come on, Dad,
Let's go here!
That is a baby ride!
Let's go to this ride,
It looks fun.

Callum Leitch (8)
Kilchrenan Primary School, Taynuilt

WINTER GRITTER

Freezing frenzy,
Greasy grit,
Mental machine,
Stupid snow,
Large load,
High hills,
Slushy snow,
Splattering snow.

Calum Galbraith (9)
Kilchrenan Primary School, Taynuilt

A ROLLER COASTER RIDE

Rush, rush, push, 'Get on, get on!'
Buckle up now and off we boost!

Up, up, down, deeper down,
Down, up, up, further up.

Sideways, backwards, down big burrows,
Upside-down and through little tunnels!

Loop-the-loops, through big hoops,
Further and further the roller coaster travels.

Oh no! Suddenly we're at the start again,
Here we go!

Up, up, down, deeper down,
Down, up, up, further up.

Sideways, backwards, down big burrows,
Upside-down and through little tunnels.

Loop-the-loops, through little hoops,
Further and further the roller coaster travels.

We've come to an end, round a bend!
Off we go, yippee and hullabaloo!

Jade Sutherland (10)
Kilchrenan Primary School, Taynuilt

CHRISTMAS TIME

Christmas is the time of year
When we shout and give a cheer
Lots of presents there for you and me
Silver tinsel on the Christmas tree

Rudolph's nose is very bright
It shines like a bright light
When we all go out to play
It is a very Christmassy day

At night, the sleigh bells ring
And Rudolph sings joyful things
Santa brings wonderful toys
To all of the nice girls and boys.

Dylan Baty (8)
St Andrew's RC Primary School, Falkirk

MY SISTER, AOIFE

My sister looks like a little angel,
Her hands are like five little pencils sticking out,
Her face is a ball with eyes, a nose and a mouth,
Her eyes are like two twinkling diamonds,
Her clothes are pink, soft and squishy like dough,
She moves like an electric train,
She walks like a jumping kangaroo,
She runs like a racing dog,
She thinks like a monkey looking for bananas,
She makes me laugh.

Amy Doyle (9)
St Andrew's RC Primary School, Falkirk

The Beautiful Killer

See the fierce eagle scan the lonely land,
Spying for food over windswept sand.
He works alone, not in a band,
Majestically he lands, trying to stand.
His razor-sharp talons killing his prey,
Enjoying his catch on this fine summer's day.

Aidan Buhrmann (8)
St Andrew's RC Primary School, Falkirk

The Hunter

Here he stands, his talons clasped tightly to the jagged crag
He is scanning the land beneath him for his next victim
His beautiful feathers shine with the bright winter's sun
Suddenly - a movement down below catches the eagle's sharp eyes
He sweeps down like an arrow and catches his prey.

Claire Williamson (9)
St Andrew's RC Primary School, Falkirk

The Killer

The powerful creature clasps his claws around the cragg,
His demon, evil, deadly eyes scan over the heather
Searching for his prey,
The fierce predator sits and waits,
He waits, his sleek, golden feathers ruffle while the wind blows,
And in a flash he has his prey clasped in his razor-sharp claws,
The razor-sharp talons rip the victim to shreds.

Mairead Cowling (9)
St Andrew's RC Primary School, Falkirk

HOLDING MY BABY SISTER, SUZANNE

My baby sister lies peacefully in my arms,
She is so delicate and fragile,
She looks so cute and loveable
And smells so fresh and clean
As if she has been in a bath.

As I hold my baby sister,
She starts to murmur,
I am scared if I drop this precious bundle,
She is so warm and soft as she is resting.

I feel proud that I have a baby sister,
My mum and dad are delighted,
Thank you God for this treasured child,
Thank you for this little baby, Suzanne.

Rachel Doherty (9)
St Andrew's RC Primary School, Falkirk

CHRISTMAS!

C hristmas is that time of year,
H oliday! So give a cheer,
R eally fun in every way,
I cy and cold, the perfect day,
S anta brings lots of toys,
T o all the little girls and boys,
M ary and her little son,
A ll of us have lots of fun,
S ince all the hard work has been done.

Ruth McElroy (8)
St Andrew's RC Primary School, Falkirk

CHRISTMAS TIME

Christmas is the time of year,
Time to spread some festive cheer.
The icy paths are all aglow,
So build a snowman in the snow.
The white icing on the cake,
Didn't take us long to make.
Look at the tinsel on the tree
And the presents there for you and me.
We all have lots and lots of fun,
When all the hard work has been done.
Santa's coming! Hip hip hooray,
We'll all have fun on Christmas Day.

Carolyn Paterson (8)
St Andrew's RC Primary School, Falkirk

CHRISTMAS IS HERE!

Christmas is the time of year
When we are full of fun and cheer
Santa Claus is coming to all the girls and boys
To bring us beautiful cuddly toys

So we go sledging, oh it's so fun!
All the hard work has been done
The reindeer have gone home, now they can rest
The robins too can make their nest.

Liam Bruce (8)
St Andrew's RC Primary School, Falkirk

HANNAH'S CHRISTMAS POEM

C is for candles on the Christmas tree,
H is for happiness for you and me,
R is for Rudolph with a big red nose,
I is for ice nipping at my toes,
S is for snow making us shiver and shake,
T is for time to make a Christmas cake,
M is for going to Mass when we awake,
A is for the angel on the top of the tree,
S is for Santa coming with glee.

Hannah Jamieson (8)
St Andrew's RC Primary School, Falkirk

CHRISTMAS IS COMING

C andles on the Christmas tree.
H appiness for you and me.
R udolph with his big red nose.
I ce and frost are on our toes.
S now makes us shiver and shake.
T ime to have a little break.
M ass we go to when we awake.
A ngel on the Christmas tree.
S anta has presents for you and me.

Claire Callaghan (8)
St Andrew's RC Primary School, Falkirk

Christmas Time

Christmas is the time of year
When girls and boys wake up with cheer
When we're out, we shout and say
'Christmas is here, so come and play!'

Girls and boys can't wait for their toys
So they listen out for the special noise
He shouts, 'Ho! Ho! Reindeer go!'
When travelling over the lovely white snow

Red stockings hanging on the wall
Last year I heard Santa fall
Merry Christmas to all of you
Celebrate and party too!

Sean Cowell (8)
St Andrew's RC Primary School, Falkirk

The Hillside Hunter

She is the ultimate predator,
She roams the Highlands.
Her talons are so sharp they cut into the rock.
She has a keen eye
And is on the lookout for her next victim.
Spotting her victim, she swoops like a speeding bullet.
Her golden, gleaming wings are used to swoop in for the kill.

Gavin Cullen (9)
St Andrew's RC Primary School, Falkirk

The Soaring Predator

He grips rock with razor-sharp claws,
Waiting, watching for his prey.
He soars around in the fresh air,
His golden feathers sparkle in the morning sun,
Something moves –
He speeds in for the kill.

Dominic Hamilton (9)
St Andrew's RC Primary School, Falkirk

The Tablet
(In memory of Alexander Fleming)

The round tablet that has saved the many lives of sick
                                            and homeless people
The round tablet that has cured the illnesses of many
The round tablet that has helped families stay together
The round tablet!

The white tablet that has helped people stay alive
The white tablet that helps people stick together as one
The white table that was a bright idea
The white tablet!

The great tablet that has cured the lives of many
The great tablet that if not invented we would die easily
The great tablet which makes lives stay together
The round tablet
The white tablet
The great tablet!

Lauren Douglas (11)
St John's Primary School, Ayr

THE MOUNTAIN TROLL

In his cave
Up in the mountain
Quiet and still
Until
The hundred dwarves come by
With pointed spears
To kill!

To kill!
The mountain troll
Is what they want
But this could not happen
For the mountain troll is fast
And the dwarves are slow
So this might never happen

It will not ever happen
But this time it is different
For the mountain troll is old
They may be able to catch him
He runs and runs
But suddenly falls
So the dwarves take him away

They take him away
And open him up
The feast begins soon
They roast him and toast him
Until he's done
As they serve the meat
The feast is done!

Rebecca Shields (11)
St John's Primary School, Ayr

CHRISTMAS

Cold snow freezing your nose
Glistening lights in windows
Christmas trees standing tall
Decorations everywhere
Presents, different shapes and sizes
Hiding under trees
Santa coming with Rudolph
Milk and cookies ready
Snowmen standing, white and tall
Everybody have a ball.

Sarah Hainey (11)
St John's Primary School, Ayr

MY AUTUMN POEM

Autumn, autumn, it's so much fun,
I love it because Christmas is coming,
Robin redbreasts are out,
Leaves are in a bundle and I jump in them,
But I have to say they are nice colours,
Bare trees are everywhere.

But now for the bad things about autumn,
Summer is nearly over,
Flowers are nearly dead,
I can't get into my car because the doors are all frosty,
When I start walking down from school
I hear the crunch of the leaves under my feet,
Then at night I hear the wind howling
And blowing the leaves about all night long.

Lewis Mair (9)
St Mark's Primary School, Hamilton

MY SPECIAL FAMILY MEMBER

My uncle Paul
Plays with me
He has red hair with no freckles
He does not like washing the dishes
But loves lying in his bed
My uncle Paul is so, so funny

My uncle Paul
Plays everything I want to play
He is tall
He hates noise when he is in his bed
But loves watching football on the TV
My uncle Paul laughs a lot

My uncle Paul
Takes me out
He always smiles
He hates trailing muck into the house
But he really likes reading 'Lord of the Rings'
My uncle Paul makes me sad because he does not like me
Going in his room to mess it up.

Brogan McKendrick (8)
St Mark's Primary School, Hamilton

MY LIFE

See the other maids moving quickly to the master's order.
Hear the master shouting for whatever he desires.
Smell the soup while I wash
And the hot meals that the cook is making.
Taste the soup from the bucket.
I feel tired and sad as the years go on.

Ami Smith (11)
St Mark's Primary School, Hamilton

My Special Family Member

My wee cousin, Ewan is cool,
He has brown hair with no freckles.
He just hates shopping,
But he loves videos,
Ewan is funky.

My wee cousin, Ewan
Lets me play video games,
He is also small,
He hates to tidy his bedroom,
But he loves eating sweets,
My cousin is good at video games.

My wee cousin, Ewan is the best,
He runs mad when he sees me,
He hates going to bed early,
But loves playing with me.
My wee cousin, Ewan plays games,
Which I do not like!

Jonathan Lennon (9)
St Mark's Primary School, Hamilton

Cleaning The Streets

See everybody rushing around and giving money to road sweepers.
Hear all of the horse and carts clattering and racing on the muddy road.
Smell the waste the horses leave behind them as they thunder past.
Touch the hard wood of my dirty old broom.
Taste the horrid smoke in the air, escaping from the tall chimneys.
I feel tired and hungry.

Stuart McPherson (9)
St Mark's Primary School, Hamilton

MY DREAM POEM

My big, smart, shiny, gold box
On my window legs
Stores things that open and shut
And gives me bad dreams

My big, gold, gorgeous box
With a lovely pattern
Brings my dad
To my dreams

My old box
Takes us to an old house
We hear
A poltergeist
I see
Freddie Kruger

My old box
Which makes me feel scared
And brings memories of
Sad times.

Charles Kirk (10)
St Mark's Primary School, Hamilton

TRAPPED

See the dark as black as night.
Hear the clanging of the pick hitting the jagged metal wall.
Smell sweaty, dirty men working for survival.
Taste the dusty, dingy rot of coal.
Touch the stone-cold trapdoor.
I feel like a mouse, scared to death.

Suzanne Hunt (11)
St Mark's Primary School, Hamilton

Autumn Poem

In autumn I see a lot of leaves on the ground
And it's like walking on a carpet of leaves.
In autumn I see dark clouds,
In autumn I hear wind blowing the bare trees
And leaves rustling when I walk through them.

In autumn I smell the bark of the tree,
Another thing I smell is the bonfire,
When people are burning the dead leaves and plants,
In autumn I taste the cold air and the bonfire.

In autumn I touch conkers,
Because I am going to play the game of conkers.
I dislike autumn because it's cold
And leaves are scattered about like litter.

Michael McMonagle (10)
St Mark's Primary School, Hamilton

A Life Underground

See the black coal as it falls on my head.
Hear the children getting whipped for being slow.
Smell the black, dusty coal clogging up my nose.
Taste the coal dust in my mouth.
Touch the rusty wagon wheels as I pull it uphill.
I feel bruised and battered.

Scott Hart (11)
St Mark's Primary School, Hamilton

Autumn

In autumn I see a dusky, pink sky,
Burgundy leaves and gold leaves like a shining sunray,
I hear the gentle sound of rustling leaves
And the lightly sprinkling rain.

I smell the bark from the trees,
The leaves lightly float to the ground,
I feel the frost on my lips
And my cold, white, smoky breath.

I touch the falling acorns
And the fire-coloured leaves in autumn,
I feel love and warmth in my heart for my family,
For my friends and especially my three grans,
Whom I think of every day.
That's why I think autumn is so magical.

Colette McKale (10)
St Mark's Primary School, Hamilton

The Dark Tomb

See the dark tomb only a wagon and me.
Hear only *bang, bang, bang,* of the spade.
Smell the smoke and dust of the mine.
Taste the smoke and gas each day.
Touch the muck and slimy dirt.
I feel the tiredness and sleepiness every single day.

Martin Scott (10)
St Mark's Primary School, Hamilton

AUTUMN

I can see bare branches
And lots of different coloured leaves.
I can hear the whistling of the wind
And the rustling of the trees.

Roasting chestnuts on a smoky bonfire,
Melting marshmallows, steaming hot chocolate,
Hot dogs, baked potatoes,
All cooked by the fire.

Crunchy leaves underfoot, covered in frost.
Puddles you can splash in, jumping all around.
I love Hallowe'en, dressing in gowns.
Best of all is Bonfire Night,
Fireworks making great sounds.

Mark Russell (9)
St Mark's Primary School, Hamilton

MY LIFE DOWNSTAIRS

Hear the giggles of the rich people entertaining.
Smell the fine food at breakfast, lunch and dinner.
See the glory and wealth of those upstairs.
Taste the lovely scraps of leftover food.
Touch the warm beds and silken sheets.
I feel warm but exhausted.

Stephanie Kirkwood (11)
St Mark's Primary School, Hamilton

THAT'S LIFE

See the dust resting on the cold floor, children darting all around.
Hear the roar of the loom and the piercing screech of steel.
Smell dampness and saltwater of the Clyde left by the bucket boys.
Taste the dust and thick fluff filling my chest, suffocating me.
Touch the pulsating rails as the loom thunders on.
I feel weak and scared.

Michael McGuckin (12)
St Mark's Primary School, Hamilton

A SWEEPER'S LIFE

See mysterious people every day wandering back and forth.
Hear horses and noisy carriages trotting all around.
Smell the cloudy smoke coming from the huge mills early
                                                        in the morning.
Taste the salty air drifting up from the Thames.
Touch the tough bristles of my brush.
I feel as if the day will never end.

Danielle Bryant (10)
St Mark's Primary School, Hamilton

NO CHOICE

See nothing, just darkness and wagons.
Hear children pulling the coal up the hill.
Smell sweat and wax dripping from my only light.
Taste the choking dust going into my dry mouth.
Touch the cold metal rails and the rough cold coal.
I feel I will never get out.

Grant Kelly (10)
St Mark's Primary School, Hamilton

My Special Family Member

My little sister, Emily cheers me up by laughing.

She has red hair and is beautiful,
She doesn't like me not paying attention to her.
My little sister loves me singing to her.
My little sister, Emily is funny and gorgeous.

My little sister, Emily lets me hold her sometimes.

She has blue eyes and a lovely face,
She has toys to play with but loves her jars of food,
Her rice and her bottles.
My little sister, Emily makes me laugh.

Linzi Carty (10)
St Mark's Primary School, Hamilton

The Road Sweeper

See the wild horses thrashing ever closer.
Hear the chatter of people as I brush the street.
Smell the rotten manure below my unwashed feet.
Taste the sweat and grime as the horses pass by.
Touch my broken broom and get splinters every day.
I feel as vulnerable as a newborn kitten.

Charlie Reilly (11)
St Mark's Primary School, Hamilton

My Autumn Poem

Falling leaves from the naked trees,
Flaming leaves lying on the icy ground,
Blowing leaves from the howling wind,
Robin's chest like a flaming hot leaf.

Smoky air from the burning wind,
Damp wood from the rain,
Freezing air from the frost,
The bark of wood from a tree.

Crunchy leaves from the ground,
Dripping water from the trees,
I love Hallowe'en,
I love bonfires,
I just love autumn.

Mark Lennon (9)
St Mark's Primary School, Hamilton

Victorian Road Sweeper

See rich people asking me to sweep the roads so they don't get dirty.
Hear the constant noise of people begging for food.
Smell smoke from the chimneys.
Taste the salt air drifting from the water.
Touch my old, long, trusty broom.
I feel very sad.

Christopher Brownlie (10)
St Mark's Primary School, Hamilton

Autumn

I see lots of naked trees
And lots of people raking,
I hear the wind blowing
And the branches shaking.

I smell lots of fires
And lots of smoke,
I can taste fog in my mouth
And I am starting to choke.

I can touch wet, soggy grass
And crinkled-up leaves
And I like autumn,
Because of all the trees.

Leigh-Ann Todd (9)
St Mark's Primary School, Hamilton

My Autumn Poem

In autumn I see steam on windows,
Acorns falling from the sky.
I watch the leaves fly.
I hear the whistling in the wind,
Leaves crunching when I step on them.

I smell the dampness
And the smoke from the night's bonfires.
I taste the fog that sits on my lips.
I touch a very cold tree and my hands freeze.
I feel autumn is very cold but I love it.

Kayleigh Currie (10)
St Mark's Primary School, Hamilton

MY AUTUMN POEM

Children playing with leaves,
The wind blowing my hair,
The whistling of wind and children laughing in my ear,
The rain on my umbrella, *tip tap, tip tap.*

I can smell the dampness of rain on the ground,
The leaves re so soggy, red and brown,
The wind slapping my lips so fresh, but cold.

I can touch my woolly hat,
Gloves and scarf keep me nice and warm,
But autumn is dull, cold and dark,
Summer I think is the best.

Lauren Steven (9)
St Mark's Primary School, Hamilton

THE HUT

See the wood and the brown wooden door
And the old, stuck, broken latch on the hut.
Hear the door and the latch and the brush sweeping,
The tree outside rocking and the pole moving.
Smell the wood and the door and the toilet that is leaking.
Touch the wood and the toilets and the brush and the wall.
Taste the smell of the brush and the wood
And the pole and the toilet leak.
I feel this is horrible.

Luke Hill (11)
St Mark's Primary School, Hamilton

My Favourite

Winter

When I think of winter,
I think of snow, snowmen, icicles,
Hats, gloves and sitting by the nice warm fire.
The thing I like best about winter is
When I get cold I know that soon it will snow
And I can go outside to play in it.
My favourite activities in winter
Are making snowmen and having a snowball fight
With Adam, my wee brother.

Summer

Whenever I think of summer,
I think of warm sand, the sun,
Ice lollies, shorts, T-shirts
And putting your feet in cold water.
The best thing about summer is
Going on holiday and playing in the sand.
My favourite activities in summer
Are building sandcastles
And playing tennis in the back garden.

Natalie Webster (10)
St Mark's Primary School, Hamilton

Fun In The Snow

We had three days of snow,
But then it had to go,
We wanted to play
And we wanted it to stay,
But the rain washed it all away!

Sarah Tait (8)
Sandbank Primary School, Dunoon

I Asked My Mum

I asked my mum to kiss my thumb,
She missed my thumb and kissed my tum.
She sang me to sleep
And I didn't make a peep.
My dream was to Mars
And I saw lots of stars.
When I woke up,
My mum had a cup.
The cup was full of water,
My mum said, 'Hello daughter.'
I drank my water
And I felt much hotter.

Kiri Newbery (9)
Sandbank Primary School, Dunoon

War Is A Bloody Battle

Swords are clashing,
Swords are bashing,
Arrows are firing,
Arrows are whizzing,
Axes are swinging,
Axes are chopping,
Daggers are cutting,
Daggers are killing,
Blood is gushing,
Blood is streaming,
This is a bloody battle.

Alexander Pearson (8)
Sandbank Primary School, Dunoon

I Wonder

I wonder why the grass is green
And why the wind is never seen?

Who taught the birds to build a nest
And told the trees to take a rest?

When the moon is not quite round,
Where can the missing bit be found?

Who lights the stars when they blow out
And makes the lightning flash about?

Who paints the rainbow in the sky
And hangs the fluffy clouds so high?

Why is it now, do you suppose,
That Dad won't tell me if he knows?

Vahri McGeoch (9)
Sandbank Primary School, Dunoon

The Cat And The Rat

There was a ginger cat,
Who sat on a muddy mat,
Speaking to a ragged rat,
Wearing a woolly hat.
The rat said to the ginger cat,
'Do you like that muddy mat?'

Emma McDougall (8)
Sandbank Primary School, Dunoon

COLOURS

Red is like a red, red rose.
Apricot is like the skin.
Indigo is like the petals on a violet.
Navy is like our school top.
Blue is like the sea.
Orange is like the fruit.
White is like sparkling snow.

Simon McVicar (8)
Sandbank Primary School, Dunoon

WHAT IS A GRAPE?

A grape is bright, shiny green,
It is sweet with an appley smell,
It tastes juicy and succulent,
It has a smooth, soft skin,
I just love grapes!

Owen James (9)
Sandbank Primary School, Dunoon

GOING TO THE MOON

There was a young girl from Dunoon,
Who wanted to go to the moon,
She jumped in her car,
Drove long and far,
But ended up staying in Troon.

Kirstin Campbell (8)
Sandbank Primary School, Dunoon

A Man Fro Inveraray

There was a man from Inveraray
who lived in a house with a big canary.
He was 49 years old
and was always cold.
He wore his jacket all night long
and kept warm by singing a song.
In the morning when the day was dawning,
he couldn't stop yawning.
When he got up,
he broke his cup.
Then he went to his garden shed
and a hammer fell on his head.
When he came to,
the day was nearly through.

Donna McFarlane (10)
Sandbank Primary School, Dunoon

Friendly Match

        T O Morrow
C Eltic   W Ill   W In
    T He   Mat C
      Heasily

     R Angers
  W Ont   S Tand
A   Chance   A Gain
    S T Us.

Conor Gillan (9)
Sandbank Primary School, Dunoon

PETER PAN

There was a man called Peter Pan
He hit his head on a frying pan
His head was sore
He fell on the floor
He began to snore
A pup came in the door
When he work up
The pup was licking a dirty cup
He got up, he felt funny
He could not find his money
He felt weird
So he decided to shave his beard
Then he felt fine
Apart from his spine
He went to bed
But banged his head
His head turned red
And then he was dead!

Ged Preston (10)
Sandbank Primary School, Dunoon

DOGS

D aydreaming all day long.
O bserving the cars as they pass by.
G oing to get some doggy treats.
S leeping, snoozing, snoring, *zzzzz!*

Mairi Tait (9)
Sandbank Primary School, Dunoon

THUNDER, THUNDER

Thunder, thunder
In the dark.
Thunder, thunder
In the park.
Thunder, thunder
In the mountains.
Thunder, thunder
In the fountains.
Thunder, thunder
In my eyes.
Thunder, thunder
In the sky.
Thunder, thunder
Under my bed.
Thunder, thunder
Get out of my head!

Tiffany Robinson (9)
Sandbank Primary School, Dunoon

THE ALIEN

There once was an alien called Ark
Who drank slime juice in the dark
He ate gungy slugs and cake
On the end of a snake
He fell asleep on a bench
And woke up in a trench
He flew back to space
And went to his own place.

Camilla Smith (9)
Sandbank Primary School, Dunoon

THE CLAN MACDUFF

The clan MacDuff
were very rough.
They got into fights
wearing their tights.
They were not a pretty sight
with tears in their tights.
People came from everywhere
to watch, stand and stare.
They all wanted to see their tights.
These tights were so bright
they lit up the night.
Nowadays if you look up in the sky
you will see these tights
in the Aurora Borealis.

Ryan Scott (10)
Sandbank Primary School, Dunoon

THE STORM

The storm is thundering which makes it frightening
I am frowning
And my dog is growling
I lie low upon the floor
While there is a strange clatter at the door
I feel like crying
While my brain is flying
Silence!
I think of the question
Why do storms use so much *violence?*

Andrew Gault (9)
Sandbank Primary School, Dunoon

SOME MUMS

Some mums are grumpy
Others are funky
Some mums are glad
Some are just plain bad
Some mums are mad
And some are even madder
Some mums are neat
And some are really sweet
Some mums are crazy
And some are very lazy.

Gemma Dorward (10)
Sandbank Primary School, Dunoon

LIGHTNING

Lightning crashing through the air,
But I didn't really care!
So I sat in my old blue chair
And started to eat and crunch,
A big chunky chocolate bar,
Then I played with my toy teddy
And his name is last in the race, Freddy.
The storm was like my angry mother,
Shouting at my big brother.
Suddenly the lightning stopped
And my favourite balloon popped.

Iona McNab (9)
Sandbank Primary School, Dunoon

YETI

There was a mountain yeti
Who loved eating beans and spaghetti
When the yeti ate candy
He felt really dandy
He loved stuffing his face
And his table manners were a disgrace
His home was in Tibet
And he liked getting wet
People said that he was abominable
And climbers thought him horrible
He still lives in the mountains
And he still drinks from water fountains
Always a snowman
Abominable
Free!

Callum Barr (8)
Sandbank Primary School, Dunoon

MONSTERS

M onsters, monsters everywhere
O n my bedroom wall
N ineteen
S cary monsters
T errifying, terrorising
E ating
R evolting, disgusting
S isters.

Liam Jaques (10)
Sandbank Primary School, Dunoon

TOFFEE, THE WINDY WELSH PONY

T oronto Toffee
O ff like a shot
F leeing the field
F aster than a trot
E fficiently he gallops
E normous belly, just like jelly.

Briony Docherty (11)
Sandbank Primary School, Dunoon

COOL SCHOOL

Come to school, it is very cool.
Don't miss school, you'll be a fool.
You learn lots of stuff and can play blind man's buff.
We play at break and learn all day long.
So come to school, don't be a ghoul.
Learning's fun for everyone, so don't miss school.
Come to school, it is very cool!

Jenny Jaques (11)
Sandbank Primary School, Dunoon

STORM

S torm raging, hailstones crashing,
T hunder rumbling,
O live trees smashing,
R ain lashing,
M agnetism smashing.

Cara Phillips (10)
Sandbank Primary School, Dunoon

NATURE ON EARTH

Have you ever heard the birds singing in the trees?
Have you ever been outside when there's a cool, relaxing breeze?
Have you ever seen a rainbow forming over the hills?
Have you ever seen a hedgehog with its spiky quills?

As I looked around, I felt a joy inside
Then I felt great and I was glad to be alive.

Have you ever been in the flowers where there are buzzy bees?
Have you ever been there when the sun is rising o'er the seas?
Have you ever tasted a strawberry, freshly picked from the field?
Have you ever smelt the fragrance of an orange that's just been peeled?

I sat down in my armchair and started to stare
And then I realised what was really there
It was the world and its nature and I started to know
That if the world and my heart would have to part,
Then my whole life would go.

Have you ever seen a butterfly open its wings?
Have you ever seen the beauty and wonder of oh, so many things?
Have you ever seen the forests and the spring green hills?
Have you ever seen a fish swimming with its shiny scales and gills?

Spring, summer, autumn, winter, all the seasons of the year
I looked outside and through all the things I'd seen,
It suddenly became clear

Was the Earth really made by the 'big bang'
Or was it made by God's creating hands?

Emily Fairclough (10)
Sandbank Primary School, Dunoon

Sunrise, Sunset

Up it comes in the morning,
Down it goes at night,
It gives you a startle,
It gives you a fright,
Its bright colours, beautiful to see,
I'm not sad,
I'm as happy as can be,
But as the day draws to a close,
The sun goes down,
My heart goes.

Stuart Gilmer (11)
Sandbank Primary School, Dunoon

Sweet Sam, My Guinea Pig

Colour of snow, coal and pine,
He has a pink ear, colour of mine.
Carrots are a favourite,
Apples too
And he's trained when he needs the loo.

To him I'm his mummy
And when he sleeps, he thinks of food.
Yummy, yummy.

He dreams of carrots,
Apples galore,
Imagining more and more and more.
Mountains of grass, hills of hay,
He wants to come in his dreams another day.

Sophie Elder (10)
Skipness School, Tarbert

UNCLE CAM'S

I love going to
My uncle Cam's,
I like to help him
With the lambs.

Staying up late,
To watch Titanic,
To see Kate,
That's so romantic.

Dogs are barking,
I'm trying to sleep,
What's that racket
In my sleep?

Uncle Cam shouting,
Dogs stop barking,
I hear a bang,
The window is shut,
Holidays are fun.

Emma Henderson (11)
Skipness School, Tarbert

My Guinea Pig

Colour of toffee,
All fat and brown,
Marked with a stripe,
Like milky coffee.

A creak of the cage door,
A patter on the kitchen floor,
Carrots with flavour
Are something to savour.

He likes me,
It's easy to see,
I like him,
By the way he's Tom not Tim.

He's in the garden at the west,
Snuggled in hay to make a nest,
For a nice warm place
That he can rest.

Aimee Elder (11)
Skipness School, Tarbert

A Fantasy Land

Once there was a fantasy land
And on that land
There was a brass band
And the person that played that great brass band
Did not come from the fantasy land.

He did not come from the fantasy land,
He came from the north,
He came from the south,
He came with a corn stalk in his mouth.

The fantasy land
Was not in the north
And not in the south,
Fantasy land as you've almost guessed,
Is of course,
In the west!

Jenny Richmond (10)
Skipness School, Tarbert

Tractor

Tractors are big, tractors are small,
Off we go to get the trailer,
Hitch it on
And off we go, down to the beach.
But it's very rough sitting in the trailer,
Load up the sand
And off we go again,
Big, powerful and smart,
That's my dad's tractor.

John Bateman (9)
Southend Primary School, Campbeltown

SCHOOL

School is good when it's art
School is good when it's maths
School is good when it's playtime
School is good when it's lunch
Especially when Jen, our dinner lady is cooking

School is bad when it's spelling
School is bad when it's grammar
School is bad when it's dictionary
School is bad when it's Monday
Especially getting up in the morning

School is OK when it's worksheets
School is OK when it's drama
School is OK when it's computer
School is OK when it's project
I suppose school is OK most of the time.

Ashleigh MacMillan (9)
Southend Primary School, Campbeltown

FUNNY BUNNY

I have got a funny little bunny
And his name is Sooty
I called him that because he is black
And he is big and furry
He is funny when he munches his food
And his fur is so smooth
He sometimes eats out of my hand
Then sometimes he gives me a little nip
But it doesn't really hurt at all
Sometimes he gets up to mischief
But he is still a funny little bunny.

Stuart McConnachie (10)
Southend Primary School, Campbeltown

Bubbles

It's 10am,
I run the bath, put in bubbles and climb in.
The water's warm,
I get some bubbles in my hand
And blow them.
They fly up, up into the air
And come back down.
I get out of the bath and get my clothes on,
I go outside and blow bubbles out of my bubble wand.
I'm blowing a big one, it gets bigger and bigger,
Now it's really big.
I call Mum, she comes running,
But suddenly, *pop!*
Oh no!
Mum tells me to come inside and get my breakfast,
I'd rather be blowing bubbles outside.

Carlyn MacMillan (10)
Southend Primary School, Campbeltown

My Dad's Lorries

I'm in my dad's lorry
I see everything
I see other lorries
They look huge

I hear the revs going down when we go up a hill
I hear the horn when we meet one of our lorries
I hear the retarder going on, going around corners

I feel tall because of the height we are at
It is so high, it's like being in a plane
My dad's lorries are the best.

Craig McKerral (11)
Southend Primary School, Campbeltown

MY ROOM

My room is big and lilac
It has blue curtains
I feel absolutely snuggled
I feel really cosy
And I feel so relaxed
Then my brother comes in
And annoys me
I'm really cross at him
Then my mum comes up
And says to my brother
'Leave her alone!'
After that I fall straight to sleep.

Natalie Smith (10)
Southend Primary School, Campbeltown

MY DREAM

I met a mermaid
I met a whale
I met a fish with a big fat tail

I found some treasure
I found some gems
I found a chest full of lovely jewels

I looked for starfish
I looked for crabs
I looked for lobster
In my dreams last night.

Karen Semple (11)
Southend Primary School, Campbeltown

UNTIDY ROOM

Here I am in my messy room,
Mum said it looks like a pigsty,
But I think when it's messy, it's cosy
And she shouts at me to tidy my room up.
'Jason! Come and tidy this room up!'
'Och! But I like it messy.'
'Too bad,' says Mum.
I tidy up.
Mum will be pleased, but I'm not.
'Jason, why is this room still like a pigsty?'
My cat lurks behind the curtains,
Looking guilty.
'Och, Tie, why did you do it?'
Miaow . . .

Jason Graham (9)
Southend Primary School, Campbeltown

WHEN I GROW UP

When I grow up, I'll be famous,
Playing for Rangers, scoring goals,
But I'll be much more than that,
I'll be better than David Beckham,
I'll be richer too!
But I can't leave out my family,
£100 would probably do.
I'll be transferred to Milan
Or maybe Real Madrid,
Wherever I go,
I'll be happy,
As long as I'm playing football.

Calum Houston (10)
Southend Primary School, Campbeltown

THE FOX

He tiptoes through the forest
Hunting for his food.
A fine red tail like a brush
And his feet as light as can be.
Soft, silent,
The trees rustling about.
As he wanders through the dark wood,
The wind is whistling all around,
But the fox is not afraid.

Then suddenly, he spies a rabbit
Out of the corner of his bright eyes.
He creeps up to it,
Silently, on his four little paws.
Then he takes a big leap,
Jumping straight onto the unsuspecting creature.
He picks it up with his sharp teeth,
Wandering back to his den,
He thinks of his delicious meal.

Rosie Fraser (9)
Southend Primary School, Campbeltown

No, Cara!

Ouch!
No, Cara! You're so heavy,
My fluffy alarm clock jumps on me,
Delivering a big, hot, wet tongue all over my face.
No, Cara! Give me my duvet back,
Ouch!
You don't need to push me out of bed,
I will not give up, I can't let a dog win!
Oh no, Cara!
I won't have any face left if you keep on licking me,
OK! OK! I'm getting up,
Where are my glasses?
No, Cara! Give me my sock!
'Mum, Dad, Cara's attacking me!'
OK! OK! Cara, let's go downstairs then,
I never knew having a puppy was so much hard work,
Especially in the morning!

Rachel Forrest (10)
Southend Primary School, Campbeltown

UNDER THE SEA

Under the sea is a great adventure
A giant swimming pool, very deep.
Under the sea
Is a wonderful place,
I see a mermaid beginning to leap.

Under the sea
There are lots of creatures,
Octopus, dolphin, turtle and fish,
Under the sea
It's very exciting,
A magic tortoise grants me a wish.

I look at my watch,
It's time to go,
Goodbye everyone under the sea,
I'll see you again, in my dream, I know.

Fiona McKerral (9)
Southend Primary School, Campbeltown

IN THE MORNING

In the morning, I switch the light on,
My eyes are sealed shut.
When I open them, the sun is coming up,
My bed is too warm to get out of.
I put my feet out and it is cold.
Then I slide out slowly
And I'm very sleepy.
I'm out of bed now,
I slowly walk to the bathroom.
I run some water in the sink,
Throw the water in my face,
The coldness makes me shiver and gasp!
I go and get dressed for school,
Then downstairs, have my breakfast,
Grab my bag
And go to school.

Laura Cameron (9)
Southend Primary School, Campbeltown

FOOD!

My favourite foods are
Macaroni cheese, spaghetti Bolognese,
What is for dinner?
Chicken pie, gammon steak,
Yum! Yum!
Shepherds pie, lentil soup,
What is it going to be?

My least favourite foods are
Quiche, sausage hotpot,
Oh yuck!
What is for dinner?
Hot dog! Disgusting,
I wish it was something nicer.

My favourite puddings are,
Jam tart, apple crunch,
Can't wait till lunch!
Apple crumble, tray bake,
Yum! Yum!
Caramel tart, pancake, jelly,
You can't get anything better.

My least favourite puddings are,
Creamed rice, bread and butter pudding,
Oh yuck!
Yoghurt,
Even worse,
Couldn't it be a different pudding?

Kerri McCorkindale (11)
Southend Primary School, Campbeltown